THE
BIBLE SPEAKS
ON
AGING

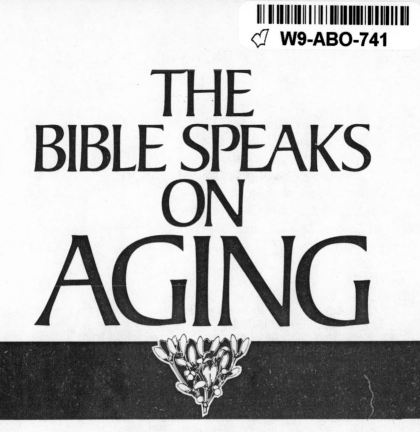

Frank Stagg

BROADMAN PRESS
Nashville, Tennessee

CONTENTS

1. Age in the Pentateuch.................... 9
2. Age in the Historical Books................. 43
3. Age in the Wisdom Books.................. 73
4. Age in the Prophets...................... 97
5. Age in the Synoptic Gospels and Acts....... 132
6. Age in the Johannie Writings.............. 142
7. Age in the Writings of Paul................ 152
8. Age in the General Epistles................ 166
9. Summary and Conclusions................. 178

Scripture quotations marked KJV are taken from the King James Version of the Bible.

Scripture quotations marked NEB are taken from *The New English Bible*. Copyright © The Delegates of the Oxford University Press and the Syndics of the Cambridge University Press, 1961, 1970. Reprinted by permission.

Scripture quotations marked TEV are taken from the *Good News Bible*, the Bible in Today's English Version. Old Testament: Copyright © American Bible Society 1976; New Testament: Copyright © American Bible Society 1966, 1971, 1976. Used by permission.

Scripture quotations marked C. B. Williams are taken from *The New Testament, a Translation in the Language of the People*, by Charles B. Williams. Copyright 1937 and 1966. Moody Press, Moody Bible Institute of Chicago. Used by permission.

Dewey Decimal Classification: 220.8
Subject heading: AGING
Library of Congress Catalog Card Number: 81-66092
Printed in the United States of America

Foreword

There has been an increasing interest by many churches and society in general in the study of and work with and for older adults. This is natural and more or less inevitable in the light of the increasing number of older adults in our society. They represent one of the most rapidly, if not the most rapidly, increasing segments of our population.

We have had in recent years, and still have to some degree, a youth movement and a woman's movement that in many ways has challenged our historic patterns of life. It is possible that we are in the beginning of an older adult "revolution" of major proportions. We do know that older adults are better organized and more vocal than ever before.

The Bible Speaks on Aging is not exclusively about or for older adults. It will, however, be of particular interest to the older adults and workers with them. It is a volume that has been needed for a long time. It is a thorough study of the Scriptures in the Old Testament and the New Testament relative to the aging process.

We are fortunate that this study was made by a recognized biblical scholar. It is a book of major significance that will be appreciated by scholars as well as lay readers. It will serve as a ready reference for many years to come. It is the type of book that one would expect from Dr. Frank Stagg.

It is a special privilege to write this brief Foreword for this book by this respected and cherished friend of mine. The longer and better I have known Frank Stagg, the greater has been my respect for him as a scholar and as a Christian friend.

T. B. MASTON

Introduction

My first serious attention to the subject of age, aging, and agism came in 1974 in response to an invitation to present a paper to the Southern Baptist Convention Conference on Aging, October 23-25, 1974, Nashville, Tennessee, under the title, "The Power and Beauty of Age." Although "age" tends to be equated with old age, everyone has a chronological age. Aging is an ongoing process which includes us all, from birth to death. Agism is any form of discrimination on the basis of age, notably against older people but actually directed against both old and young on occasion.

Significantly, this first conference on aging conducted by the Southern Baptist Convention resulted from the initiative of students from The Southern Baptist Theological Seminary who persuaded the SBC at its 1973 meeting in Portland, Oregon, to sponsor a conference on aging. On May 2, 1977, the paper (with only slight modification) was presented under the title "Biblical Perspectives on Aging" to the Clergy Seminar on Religion and Aging, Lexington Theological Seminary, Lexington, Kentucky. On October 17-21, 1977, the paper was presented to The Presbyterian Church in the United States at their First Annual Conference on Aging, in Montreat, North Carolina. In 1978 the paper was published by the General Assembly Mission Board, Presbyterian Church, United States, and the National Interfaith Coalition on Aging, Inc.

Although this book drew its original impulse from the above, it is a fresh study, more broadly based and applied. Its immediate occasion was in the initiative of the Family Ministry Department of The Sunday School Board of the Southern Baptist Convention, who proposed the production of a book and its publication through Broadman Press.

This book grew out of a fresh study of the Bible, with a careful working through it from Genesis through Revelation, putting to it the various questions bearing on age, aging, and agism. Each person has an age. We ask, "What is your age?" Often, "age" is equated with "old age," and this itself is agism. How was age perceived? How did the aged see themselves? What privileges or advantages were accorded age? What discriminations appear against age or age groups? What traces are there of "agism" — that is, bias, prejudice, stereotype, or discrimination on the basis of age? What factors enter into the aging process? Especially, how may one best prepare for old age? What if any is the correlation between age and quality of life? These and other questions were put to the biblical text throughout.

Some guidance came through such helps as the concordance, but the richest disclosures came another way. They arose directly out of the text and context, many times with no special words, such as would be found in a concordance, to give the clue. Secondary sources were consulted, but from first to last the main dependence was upon the biblical text itself, read through in its wholeness.

How to organize the book into chapters was somewhat problematic, with several viable options considered. Since many expected to use the book will do so in a church setting, it was thought best basically to follow the order to the English Bible. This is done consistently through the Old Testament. For the New Testament, the writings are gathered into four familiar groupings: the Synoptic Gospels and Acts, the Johannine writings, the Pauline writings, and the General Epistles. In the Old Testament books writings are gathered into four groups: the Pentateuch, History, Wisdom Literature, and the Prophets.

It is recognized that this is somewhat arbitrary and a convenience for publishing. Ideally, all writings would follow in their probable chronological sequence; but this was thought beyond the competence and scope of this book. Dating of books as they stand is difficult enough, with no finality within even scholarly reach. Also, within given writings seem to be discernible strata representing diverse origins, situations, and dates. For the purpose of this book it seemed best to follow the simpler plan reflected in our chapter divisions. Whatever their actual sequence, certain perspectives on age are embedded in biblical writings, and these we have sought to expose and assess.

This book has a primary concern for older people, for they are the ones who are hurt most by agism. This book is concerned with helping older people understand themselves better. It is concerned with helping younger people understand older people better and relate to them more humanely. But this book is not for older people only. Aging? That's all of us. Aging begins with birth and continues until death.

How best to grow older is a proper concern for anyone able to read this book. The quality of the older years is best determined in what we do with the younger years. Although it is never too late for one still able to make choices to do something about the older years, it is never too early to begin getting ready to be old. This book intends to speak to all ages about a most important experience common to us all—growing older. It speaks basically from biblical perspectives, with the entire Bible studied afresh for this purpose.

Unless otherwise indicated, Old Testament quotations are from the Revised Standard Version of the Bible, copyrighted 1946, 1952, © 1971, 1973. New Testament readings are in the author's translations.

1
Age in the Pentateuch

The five books surveyed in this chapter represent the oldest part of the Hebrew canon of Scriptures. They are known to the Hebrew canon as the *Torah* (Law) and are followed by "The Prophets" and "The Writings." *Pentateuch* simply designates the Torah in its fivefold character. It is beyond the purpose of this study of age and aging to enter into such debates as to whether it is better to recognize a Hexateuch (including Joshua) rather than a Pentateuch. Gathering these five books in one chapter is a convenience in chapter arrangements for our study. Each book will be treated separately. Strata within these books and stages in their development to their present form are assumed; but such analysis will not be pursued here. The fact of varied perspectives on age is apparent, whatever the sequence of their emergence or their causal factors. Our attention will be to the perspectives themselves.

Genesis

Age is a major issue in Genesis, with great significance for our study. Genesis is very age conscious, with special attention to a man's age at the time of his marriage, his fathering of his first son, and his death. Longevity is clearly viewed as positive, if not actually normal. It is short life and not long life which is abnormal. Age is not equated with wisdom or goodness, but it is readily associated with these positive qualities. On the other hand, there are several ways in which the factor of age is overridden by other factors, namely personal qualities of character or competence.

So dominating in modern thought is the limit "threescore years and ten," or possibly fourscore years of Psalm 90:10, that Genesis 6:3 is almost forgotten. It is difficult to estimate the extent to which modern attitudes and practices are dominated by Psalm 90:10. Life expectancy, retirement, and possibly in many cases death itself are to a great extent influenced by this terminus as though fixed by nature or divine decree. Genesis knows nothing about 70 as normal life expectancy. Even the 120 years specified in Genesis 6:3 represent a shortening of the normal or natural life span because of human evil. In other words, in the perspective of Genesis, one should be expected to live for centuries — not just up to 120 years and certainly not limited to 70 or 80 years.

The longevity ascribed to most of the prominent men in Genesis tests the credulity of even many of the devout whose whole disposition is to take the Bible just as it is — up to 969 years! "As old as Methuselah" is proverbial (Gen. 5:25-27); but even in his record-breaking longevity, he barely outlived numerous others. Methuselah's 969 years stagger our imagination only as we measure them against the psalmist's limit of three and a half or fourscore years and longevity as we know it, where anyone over sixty is a senior adult and anything over one hundred is world news. To Genesis, Methuselah is the "winner" in longevity, but he was not in a class to himself.

Here are the ages ascribed to men (and one woman!) in Genesis: Adam, 930 years; Seth, 912 years; Enosh, 905 years; Kenan, 910 years; Mahalalel, 895 years; Jared, 962 years; Enoch, 365 years (almost a youngster when translated!); Methuselah, 969 years; Lamech, 777 years; Noah, 950 years; Shem, 600 years; Arpachshad, 438 years; Shelah, 433 years; Eber, 464 years; Peleg, 239 years; Reu, 239 years; Serug, 230 years; Nahor, 148 years (even he exceeded the 120 limit); Terah, 205 years; Heran, the father of Lot, died at unspecified age before his father Terah; Abraham, 175 years; Sarah, 127 years; Ishmael, 137 years; Isaac, 180 years; Jacob, 147 years; and Joseph, 110 years. Of all these men and one woman (Sarah), only Joseph lived less than the 120 year limit imposed in Genesis 6:3.

However one handles the historical question, whether these extreme ages are to be taken literally or not, the perspective is clear. Genesis preserves an ancient view that human life properly extends into centuries. Interestingly, science today may have more faith in the perspective of Genesis than do religion and theology. Science is now seeking the clue to aging and does not rule out the possibility that a hormone may be discovered which will significantly modify aging. That human life could be greatly extended is not ruled out by science.[1] The time may come when the perspective of Genesis on longevity does not seem strange at all. More important, long life in Genesis is seen as good. Age is respected, not just revered. Age is itself not seen as a disqualification for responsible position in life. At the same time, long life is not itself equated with goodness, wisdom, or competence.

Equally impressive alongside the longevity

ascribed to its heroes is the normal age for the fathering of children. Adam was 130 when he fathered his first son, Seth. Seth was 105 when he fathered his first son, Enosh. So it goes: Enosh was 90 when he fathered Kenan; Kenan was 70 when he fathered Mahalalel; Mahalalel was 65 when he fathered Jared; Jared was 162 when he fathered Enoch; Enoch was 65 when he fathered Methuselah; Methuselah was 187 when he fathered Lamech; Lamech was 182 when he fathered Noah; Noah was 500 when he fathered Shem, Ham, and Japheth; Shem was 100 when he fathered Arpachshad; Arpachshad was 35 when he fathered Shelah; Shelah was 30 when he fathered Eber; Eber was 34 when he fathered Peleg; Peleg was 30 when he fathered Reu; Reu was 32 when he fathered Serug; Serug was 30 when he fathered Nahor; Nahor was a mere 29 when he fathered Terah; Terah was 70 when he fathered Abram.

Against this background, it is somewhat surprising that the birth of Isaac to Abraham at 100 and Sarah at 90 came as a surprise, at least as far as Abraham was concerned. Nothing before or after in Genesis suggests that it was unusual for a man of 100 years to become father of a child. Mothering a baby at 90 was isolated even in Genesis. The record in Genesis is that both Abraham and Sarah laughed when they heard the promise of a child to their union. When told that he would have a son by Sarah, "Abraham fell on his face and laughed, and said to himself, 'Shall a child be born to a man who is a hundred years old? Shall Sarah, who is ninety years old, bear a child?' " (Gen. 17:17). Compared to some who fathered children in the Genesis story, Abraham was rather young.

Age is relative now, and it appears to be in Genesis. How old is old? Both Abraham and Sarah saw themselves as old at 100 and 90 respectively. When promised a child, "Sarah laughed to herself, saying, 'After I have grown old, and my husband is old, shall I have pleasure?' " (18:12). Also, " 'Shall I indeed bear a child, now that I am old?' " (v. 13). The author of Genesis remarked, "Now Abraham and Sarah were old, advanced in age" (18:11). He was then 99 and Sarah 89, quite young as compared to others in Genesis. Lot's daughters agreed, " 'Our father is old' " (Gen. 19:31), but he was not too old to father their children (v. 36). Sarah saw both her husband and herself as old: " 'Who would have said to Abraham that Sarah would suckle children? Yet I have borne him a son in his old age' " (21:7).

Of Abraham at the time of his concern that Isaac have a wife it was said, "Now Abraham was old, well advanced in years" (24:1). At this time he must have been about 140, for Isaac (born to him at 100) was 40 years of age when he took Rebekah to wife (25:20). Abraham "died in a good old age, an old man and full of years" (25:8). He was 175 at death. Jacob was an "old man" when his sons first went down into Egypt to buy grain (43:27; 44:20). Jacob was then about 130 years of age, for he lived in Egypt 17 years and died at 147 (47:9,28). From his perspective, Jacob's life was short: "The days of the years of my sojourning are a hundred and thirty years; few and evil have been the days of the years of my life, and they have not attained to the days of the years of the life of my fathers in the days of their sojourning" (47:9). Compared to others, his years were short.

Probably to most people their years have been short. To others one may seem to have been here always; to oneself the tenure has been extremely brief. Of course, this does not hold for those weary of life or who have never found meaning in it. To them, a few years may seem an eternity. Which is to say, age is a relative matter.

In Genesis, gray hairs (42:38; 44:29) and poor eyesight (27:1; 48:10) are associated with old age. "When Isaac was old and his eyes were dim so that he could not see" (27:1), he could not by sight distinguish between his sons Esau and Jacob. He could still hear well enough to distinguish their voices (27:22), and he yet had a keen sense of smell (27:27). Significantly, the story does not scorn Isaac for his impairment of sight; it exposes the trickery of Jacob and his mother Rebekah. At 180 years, Isaac died "old and full of days" (35:29).

Stereotype is a major crime against senior adults as well as against most people in some way: age, sex, race, nationality, etc. Just as there is racism and sexism, there is agism—the stereotype which sees all old people as being alike and the practice of discrimination simply on the basis of age. In Genesis there is no such stereotype as to equate wisdom, character, or competence with a certain age. Two examples may be cited. When Abraham turned to the matter of securing a proper wife for his son Isaac, he delegated the mission to "his servant, the oldest of his house, who had charge of all that he had" (24:2). For Abraham nothing could be more important than ensuring his line of decendants, and he found his oldest servant to be the one to trust and employ in this mission. Age was a credential here, not a liability.

By contrast, Joseph was "a young Hebrew" (41:12) only 30 years of age (41:46) when selected to be next in power to the Pharaoh in Egypt. Anticipating a seven-year period of prosperity followed by a seven-year period of famine, Pharaoh was advised: "Now therefore let Pharaoh select a man discreet and wise, and set him over the land of Egypt" (41:33). Pharaoh posed the question thus: "Can we find such a man as this, in whom is the Spirit of God?" (v. 38). Such a man was found in the thirty-year-old Joseph: "So Pharaoh said to Joseph, 'Since God has shown you all this [disciphering visions], there is none so discreet and wise as you are; you shall be over my house, and all my people shall order themselves as you command; only as regards the throne will I be greater than you'" (vv. 39-40). Joseph, indeed, was given a position of highest responsibility: "He [God] has made me a father to Pharaoh, and lord of all his house and ruler over all the land of Egypt" (45:8). Joseph was not selected because he was young but because he had the personal credentials for the appointment.

Abraham turned to his oldest servant and Pharaoh turned to a young man of thirty. There is no suggestion that being old in one case or being young in the other was decisive. It does follow that in the perspective of Genesis the age factor can be transcended by personal factors, whether in a life of many or few years. It does follow that, other things being equal, age is considered a plus and not a minus in Genesis.

The quality of a life may improve or deteriorate with aging, depending upon the direction in which it moves. What we do with the years largely determines what the years do with us. What is decisive is not calendar years but personal qualities of attitude, values, principles, disposition, and the like. Jacob is a prime example of a life which improved with aging. In youth he was a scheming little egocentric, self-serving at the expense of his brother Esau or anyone else whom he could manipulate or exploit for selfish advantage. Only in advancing age did Jacob begin to emerge as an authentic human being, less as Jacob the schemer and more as Israel, prince of God. That the qualities which emerged in Jacob's later years were latent in his youth is probable. In the presence of God and through some traumatic experiences the latent was awakened into reality. Jacob began to emerge as "Israel" when finally he stopped running and faced himself in terms of his fear of Esau and his sins against even his own family, as he faced Esau, and as he faced God. He learned to receive (not just take), to be grateful (not just envious), and to trust God and other people (not just himself).

Jacob may serve as a reminder that it is not too late for a life to take a turn for the better as long as one is capable of exercising options. Of course, the odds are against such change, the longer delayed and the more hardened a life becomes along lines followed from youth. Jacob's late turn for the better is a reminder that any doctrine of determinism or fixed fate is to be rejected. Jacob's late conversion is an answer to Nicodemus: "How can a man be born again when he is old?" (John 3:4). Under God, such conversion is possible in the later years. It is more probable and meaningful if it occurs in the early years.

Summary. It does not follow necessarily that there is a single perspective on age in Genesis. However, age comes out extremely well throughout Genesis. Longevity is perceived as natural and normal. The shortening of the life span to 120 years is charged to human evil, not to creation or nature. To

die at an advanced age is uniformly seen as good, as
reflected in the expression "died in a good old age, an
old man and full of years" (25:8; see also 15:15; see
also 35:29). A given life span may be seen as long or
short, a matter of perspective. Age is expected to be
a credential for competence, but youth is not pre-
cluded. There is no agism in Genesis, no discrimination on the basis of age. Stereotype is avoided. There
is no necessary correlation between personal qualities and length of years. Genesis may have a cult of
age; if so, it is modified by such examples as Joseph.
It has no cult of youth, there being no hint that positive qualities belong primarily to youth.

Exodus

The preoccupation with age in Genesis makes an
exodus in the book of Exodus. In Genesis one is
almost always given the ages of the heroes: at marriage, at the time they fathered their first male child,
and at death. Longevity is normal for the heroes, and
it is seen positively as good. By contrast, age is
rarely mentioned in Exodus. However, this is to look
only at the surface. Beneath the surface, Exodus has
much to offer with respect to age and how it may be
viewed. As far as it goes, Exodus affirms age and in
no way denigrates it.

In the rare instances where ages are mentioned,
the years are many by our standards. Apparently
long life is seen positively, although this is not explicit. Levi lived 137 years, Kohath 133 years, and
Aram, the father of Aaron and Moses, 137 years.
More significantly, Moses was 80 years of age and
his brother Aaron 83 years of age when they were
commissioned to speak to Pharaoh and lead the people of Israel out of Egyptian bondage (7:7). Nothing is

said about its being an advantage or disadvantage to be an octogenarian. In all the history of Israel, no two persons were given heavier responsibilities than those two brothers, commissioned at 80 and 83. Apparently they were selected not because they were in their eighties, but because they were suited to their assignments, as is made explicit for those enlisted to construct and adorn the tabernacle (see later).

The age of Jethro is not disclosed in chapter 18, where his role in counseling Moses is described. It is noted that he was the father-in-law to Moses, so presumably he was older than the 80-year-old Moses. Jethro functioned not only as "the priest of Midian" (v. 1) but as the wise counselor to Moses, helping his son-in-law take better care not only of himself but of the people of Israel. He warned Moses of the negative results of his ill-advised zeal in trying to minister to Israel alone: "What you are doing is not good. You and the people with you will wear yourselves out, for the thing is too heavy for you; you are not able to perform it alone" (vv. 17-18). After proposing a plan for the utilization of a great number of people in a shared ministry, Jethro promised Moses: "If you do this, and God so commands you, then you will be able to endure, and all this people also will go to their place in peace" (v. 23). Not bad advice to an 80-year-old leader coming from his presumably yet older father-in-law! Moses accepted the advice and acted upon it (v. 24). By modern standards, both Moses and Jethro could have been "retired" as men "superannuated" and considered too old for such posts as the deliverer of Israel and the priest of Midian.

The prominence of Moses, Aaron, and Jethro in Exodus, all "old" men, does not justify the generalization that responsible position belongs properly to the aged alone. It is to be noted that Joshua, chief servant to Moses, is introduced as "a young man" (33:11). Some years later, Joshua succeeded Moses at the latter's death (Josh. 1:1), but it was as "a young man" that he came into prominence in the leadership of Israel. Although not explicit, Exodus would seem to view seniority as normally a plus; but it is free of such stereotype as equates eligibility or appropriateness in leadership with old age or with youth. As may be seen in the closing chapters of Exodus, suitability to a task is to be determined on relevant grounds, including spirit, motive, and ability.

Man dies; God lives on. In the opening chapters of Exodus, two basic realities are juxtaposed: all people die (1:6) and God lives on (3:6,16). Whether this is done consciously and deliberately is something the author of Exodus alone could settle for us. The two realities are brought into focus, whatever the intention: (1) "Then Joseph died, and all his brothers, and all that generation" (1:6). The death rate for human beings is one hundred percent and has been so throughout our history. (2) God said, "I am the God of your father, the God of Abraham, the God of Isaac, and the God of Jacob" (3:6). God transcends the passing generations, equally the God of parents and children, whatever the generation. God alone escapes the pattern of youth giving way to age, with death waiting somewhere down the road, whether soon or late. Any theology of age and aging needs to come under the perspective of those two realities juxtaposed in Exodus—all people die; God lives on.

Honoring father and mother. From the Ten Commandments a clear lesson is to be learned on the subject of age. The Fifth Commandment reads, "Honor your father and your mother, that your days may be long in the land which the Lord your God gives you" (20:12). The command does not necessarily imply respect for age, for parents may be quite young. Obviously, it is parenthood itself which is to be respected by children. Parents are older than their children (a truism), so there is the principle that the older is entitled to respect by the younger; but in biblical teaching, the younger also are to be respected by the older, including parental respect for children (see also Eph. 6:4; Col. 3:21). The promise "that your days may be long in the land which the Lord your God gives you" does imply that longevity is good. It would be difficult to demonstrate that respect for parenthood and longevity always are found together, for death can come early to the good while many evil people live long lives; but there is no doubt about the perspective of Exodus on length of days. Long life is esteemed as a plus, as something good to be desired; and mutual respect is on the side of longevity, not against it.

Criteria for service. Much of the latter half of Exodus (chaps. 25-40) is devoted to the making and adorning of the ark of the covenant, the tabernacle, and the high priestly robes. Careful description is given of each detail for materials that were to be used and how they were to be put together. Equal attention is given to the kind of persons who were to be employed in constructing and adorning these properties designed for worship. Significantly, the criteria for those giving the materials and those constructing and adorning them are personal, moral, and spiritual. They are matters of spirit, motive, and ability. They are not matters of chronological age or sexual identity, whether male or female. Contributions of materials and the skilled services of men and women were to be accepted on condition that persons were of right spirit, motive, and ability. There is no agism here.

Contributions were accepted from "both men and women; all who were of a willing heart" (35:22). Spinning was done by "all women who had ability" (v. 25), by "all the women whose hearts were moved with ability" (v. 26). Gifts were brought by "all the men and women, the people of Israel, whose heart moved them to bring anything for the work which the Lord had commanded ... to be done" (v. 29). A special role was assigned Bezalel, of whom it is said that God "filled him with the Spirit of God, with ability, with intelligence, with knowledge, and with all craftsmanship, to devise artistic designs, to work in gold and silver and bronze, in cutting stones for setting, and in carving wood, for work in every skilled craft" (vv. 31-33). Employment was open to "every able man in whose mind the Lord had put ability, every one whose heart stirred him up to come to do the work" (36:2).

This refrain is carried through the chapters which describe the provisions for the magnificence and beauty of the ark, the tabernacle, and the high priestly robes. Nothing is said about age, whether young or old. No age limits are given for those who would offer their gifts or their skills. The important thing about a carpenter was not how old he was but how well he could saw a board and drive a nail. The important thing about a stonemason was not the date of his birth but how well he could hew a stone. The important thing about a woman who would spin or weave was not her age but how well she could accomplish the task. Of course, qualities of character and personal spirit were primary; but these were not determined by date of birth, sexual identity, or whether one had a full head of hair or was bald.

At this point—chapter after chapter—Exodus does focus on relevant criteria for giving and serving. They also are just (fair) criteria. One does have something to do with one's spirit, motive, and character. One has nothing to do with date of birth. Matching skills to task is fair both to the task and to the people concerned. This is not to say that in Exodus there is no trace of sex or age discrimination or that the assigning of tasks on some arbitrary principle was completely overcome; but it is noteworthy that in this closing half of Exodus, in its consuming focus on the preparation of properties designed for worship, the only criteria made explicit are relevant ones: spirit, motive, and ability.

This principle reappears in the writings of Paul, in Romans 12:1-6. In his discussion of the gifts of God's grace (charismata), Paul drove home the point that the possession of a gift carries with it the obligation for its exercise. Unfortunately, in religion and in life otherwise, acceptability often is determined by criteria irrelevant to the task—criteria such as age, sex, race, or physical looks!

The elders of Israel. Frequent mention is made in Exodus of "the elders of Israel," and this surely has great significance for ancient perspective on age. The phrase is introduced without interpretation, as though established and familiar to the reader. In fact, the same holds for the introduction of the phrase or its close parallel throughout the Bible. Much remains unknown to us about the origin and meaning of "the elders" so prominent in the Bible. Probably the reason such little explanation is given is because the role(s) of "the elders" goes so far back into the ancient world, appeared so widely, and evolved so normally in the ancient world that there was no felt need for explaining it. If so, this makes it all the more significant that the ancient world, Jewish and non-Jewish, made so big a place in its civil and religious life for "the elders" as appears to be the case. It seems that "elder" first designated seniority (see below on 1 Pet. 5:1-5) and later came to designate a role or office, with no necessary reference to age.

"The elders of Israel" appear early in Exodus (3:16,18). Here they are to accompany Moses in going to the king of Egypt with the demand that he let God's people go. In 12:21 "the elders of Israel" are instructed by Moses, "Select lambs for yourselves according to your families, and kill the passover lamb." Here the elders presumably are the heads of families, the Passover, initially at least, being a family observance.[2] In 18:12 "the elders of Israel" and Aaron appear together "to eat bread with Moses' father-in-law before God." Unless an extremely large group is implied, that is, all heads of families, this may intend a more select and restricted group of elders with special authority or role closely related to that of the high priest. In 24:1,9 this becomes explicit, where God says to Moses, "Come up to the Lord, you and Aaron, Nadab, and Abihu, and seventy of the elders of Israel, and worship afar off." In 24:11 these seventy elders seem to be the same as "the chief men of the people of Israel." The formation of a body of seventy elders is explicit in Numbers 11:16, "And the Lord said to Moses, 'Gather for me seventy men of the elders of Israel, whom you know to be the elders of the people and officers over them; and bring them to the tent of meeting, and let them take their stand there with you'" (see also v. 24).

Apparently each town in Israel had its elders, whose responsibility it was to administer the civil and religious affairs of the town (see also Deut. 19:12; 21:2; Ruth 4:2-11). That such a system prevailed widely in the ancient world is attested by the presence of "the elders of Midian," "the elders of Moab," and "the elders of Gilead" (Num. 22:4,7; Judg. 11:5-11). The Jewish Gerousia (Elders) or Sanhedrin, the highest court in much of ancient Israel, is best understood against this background. Seemingly, the role of "elder" arose within the family and was extended to the towns and the nation, as senior adults were turned to for administering family, civil, and religious justice and as they were called upon to serve in various other capacities where age should be an advantage.

It appears that "elder" initially implied age, one who had attained some measure of seniority. One form of the Hebrew term designated the bearded chin of a man (Lev. 13:29; 2 Sam. 10:5; Isa. 15:2). The verb form is used for becoming old or being old (Gen. 18:12). The noun is used for an old person. The "elders of Israel" probably were older persons when the term emerged. Later its usage shifted more to the role or function with no primary reference to chronological age. A parallel to this may be seen in our term "senate," Latin for a body of senior adults. Senate and senator are no longer terms primarily designating age, although age is not entirely forgotten. A United States senator may be a young man, in his thirties. An "Elder" in a church today may be young or old. Interestingly, in a church known to me one "Elder" is a young woman in her twenties.

Although the term "Elder" has evolved in its usage, it is significant that it was first applied to senior adults whose age apparently was considered a likely advantage in counseling. That room was made for quality apart from seniority under the term "elder" is to the credit of all who at least to that extent escaped the stereotype that competence and age stand in a one-to-one relationship with one another.

The evolving of "the elders of Israel" attests to the recognition that seniority should be a dependable or at least favorable source for wisdom. The movement in the direction less inclined to equate wisdom with age but to look for competence at whatever age was most commendable. To take a further step with much modern perspective in which suitability is to be sought in youth alone is a step backward, not forward. A "cult of youth" is merely one form of agism. The biblical term "elder," like the secular term "senate," reflects a proper inclination to respect age as a likely source of wisdom. To equate age with wisdom or competence is another form of agism, and it runs into the face of the evidence that wisdom and competence do not stand in a one-to-one relationship with one's age. To exclude age in favor of youth is to make the same mistake, only in the opposite direction. The book of Exodus can remind us that the proper criteria for service are the relevant ones of spirit, motive, and ability. Age can be a factor in the cultivation of those qualities; but, as we shall see later, they may diminish or be enhanced with aging.

Leviticus

Leviticus takes one into a world distant and strange to most Christians today, and probably equally so to most Jews. A few links survive between Leviticus and modern Judaism and Christianity, but for the most part the distance is great. The twenty-seven chapters are devoted to minute description of cultic worship centering around altars, sacrifices, and priestly service. No detail is left without a rule — for example, in the preparation of a ram for priestly ordination, what to do with "the fat tail, and all the fat that was on the entrails, and the appendage of the liver, the two kidneys with their fat, and the right thigh" (8:25). Jewish piety still observes the prohibitions against the eating of whatever animals fail either to have the cloven foot or chew the cud (11:3) or whatever things taken from the waters lack either fins or scales (11:9), but Christian piety finds release from all this in a sweeping example and teaching of Jesus by which he "cleansed all foods" (Mark 7:15,19). Christian churches enjoy their catfish suppers, with clear conscience with respect to Leviticus 11. We still practice all too often the rule of "eye for eye, tooth for tooth" (Lev. 24:20) despite the teaching of Jesus to the contrary (Matt. 5:38-42); and neither Jew nor Christian lets his economics be embarrassed by the prohibition of lending money on interest (Lev. 25:35-38). What about age? Does Leviticus instruct us here?

There is little direct attention to age in Leviticus, but there are some significant passages, some explicit and some by implication. On the whole age is esteemed, with one passage susceptible to negative implications for certain age groups (27:1-8).

As in Exodus, we meet the expression "the elders of Israel" (9:1) and its parallel, "the elders of the congregation" (4:15). As in Exodus, the terms are introduced without interpretation, as though established and familiar to the reader. Presumably, these "elders" are the forerunners to the "elders" found prominent in the Jewish synagogues and in the early churches, as attested throughout the New Testament. Apparently these were lay people who exercised some roles of authority first in Hebrew families or clans and then in towns and finally in the civil and religious life of the nation. In Leviticus they are introduced in relationship with cultic worship centered in the tabernacle.

In 4:15 "the elders of the congregation" are introduced in relation to sacrificial service presided over by Aaron and the priests. In 9:1 the role of "the elders of Israel" is the same: "On the eighth day Moses called Aaron and his sons [priests] and the elders of Israel," with instructions about the offering of a bull calf as a sin offering. The role of the elders here seems to be one of assisting the priests in cultic rites, but nothing is divulged as to the origin of their office or role, and nothing is specified as to the age of "the elders." As seen above, literal age seems to have been the original reference, with usage shifting later to role itself. In any event, seniority in some sense lies behind the term, and it reflects positively on age.

The hoary head. Although somewhat isolated, in Leviticus is encountered for the first time an explicit command to respect old age: "You shall rise up before the hoary head, and honor the face of an old man, and you shall fear your God: I am the Lord" (19:32). There is no indication of at what age one is to be recognized as "an old man." Even "hoary head" does not settle it, for white or gray hair appears at various ages, from youth to many years. With all its precision in its many cultic prescriptions, Leviticus is content here simply to require respect for old age, without defining it by the calendar. "Old" is a relative term, depending upon what we are talking about; and even when applied to people, it is relative. We do not all "age" at the same rate, and stereotype is out of place here as elsewhere.

The custom of standing up in the presence of old people belonged to the cultures of many ancient people. Age was to be honored. That the privileges of age may be and actually are abused by many old people does not change the disposition deeply imbedded in history to respect old age. Other claims may override this one on occasion, but the claim of old age is there, too.

It is not clear why the fear of God is linked to honoring old age, but so it is in this passage. Possibly the only intention is to underscore the fact that respect for age is a divine command. Probably the intention is to register the fact that ultimate honor and respect belong to God alone. Old people are to be honored, but they are not to be worshiped. Old age is to be recognized as a credential, but old and young alike are to stand before God in the "fear" that is reverence. Any valid theology of youth or age must recognize that God is above us all, and to him we must make our final reckoning, including how we treat one another (see also the principle applied to slave and master in Eph. 6:9; Col. 4:1).

Valuation of age groups. The closing chapter of
Leviticus is concerned with persons and things
vowed to God and the conditions under which they
may be substituted for or redeemed. Persons could
dedicate themselves to the service of the sanctuary
or be dedicated by others, and things could be dedicated to the service of God. The passage before us
lays down conditions and procedures by which one
might be released from such vow or pledge, by the
substitution of a money payment. The provision
seems to be humanitarian in principle, intending to
provide an option and especially to ease the burden
in the case of the poor, where the priest could use his
discretion as to what should be required of one lacking the usual price for the revoking of a vow (27:8).

The point which concerns us here is not the law of
the commutation of vows but the "valuation" of persons according to age and sex. There is some ambiguity as to implications of the gradation system,
by which assessments differed according to age and
sex. The highest price for revoking a vow fell upon
males from age 20 to 60, these valued at fifty shekels. Males from 5 to 20 years were valued at twenty
shekels. Males from 1 month to 5 years were valued
at five shekels. Males above 60 years were valued at
fifteen shekels of silver. Females in each age bracket
were valued at one-half the male valuation.

Judging from the mercy shown the poor (v. 8), the
gradation for age brackets, male and female, must
have been intended to be considerate and fair. Probably from 20 to 60 were seen as the most productive
years, with males having advantage over females
economically. Least productive would be children
from 1 month to 5 years, but it is not apparent why
little girls should be less so than little boys from 1

month to 5 years. Significant is age 60 as the recognized line between the highest evaluation and that next to least. Males above 60 were valued less than 5-year-olds. Does this intend to classify them as belonging to a second childhood? The answer is not apparent, but it is difficult to escape some negative implication for old age as well as for the female at any age. Agism and sexism have had their proponents and opponents in religious practice, of old and until now.

No explanation is given here as to how age 60 was arrived at as marking the distinction between the highest valuation and next to lowest. Presumably the figure marked the beginning of "old age" to these who selected the figure. Interestingly, the Dead Sea Scrolls offer some light at this point. *The Damascus Rule*, of which extensive fragments have been found in three of the Qumran caves, contains this rule for the judges of the congregation: "No man over the age of sixty shall hold office as Judge of the Congregation" (DR X).[3] The rule limiting judgeship to age sixty is based on Jubilees, xxiii, 11, one of the outside books of the Jews dating probably from the first century BC.[4] *The Damascus Rule* cites Jubilees to this effect: "Because man sinned, his days have been shortened, and in the heat of His anger against the inhabitants of the earth God ordained that their understanding should depart even before their days are completed." These perspectives unfavorable to age thus did appear in ancient Judaism, as did perspectives favorable to age.

The book of Jubilees has an extended comment on the shortening of human life, giving an early trace of age 60 as a normal terminus for meaningful human life (Jubilees 23:1-32). The writer explains that up to the Flood "the days of the forefathers, of their life, were nineteen jubilees" (23:9). A jubilee was seven weeks of years plus one, that is, 50 years. Nineteen jubilees would be 950 years. After the Flood, so holds the writer, the life span was shortened and men grew old quickly because of their evil. He sees generations from the Flood until the coming great judgment experiencing the shortening of life: "And all the generations which shall arise from this time until the day of the great judgment shall grow old quickly, before they complete two jubilees, and their knowledge shall forsake them by reason of their old age (and all their knowledge shall vanish away)" (23:11). He goes on to say that if a man lives a jubilee and a half (75 years), it would be said of him, "He has lived long, and the greater part of his days are pain and sorrow and tribulation, and there is no peace" (23:12). He further cites "three score and ten" as normal life expectancy, as in Psalm 90:10 (23:15). Even in Jubilees, the life expectancy is about 75 years, but moral and intellectual impairment apparently are seen as beginning earlier. At least, *The Damascus Rule* sees age 60 as the terminal age for judges of the congregation. Whether that work was influenced by Leviticus 27:1-8 is not indicated.

Probably the most deplorable position taken in Jubilees is the linking of mental impairment with one's sin. Of course, one may bring upon oneself a breakdown in body and/or mind, and one's own sins may account for impairment in old age. But to generalize upon this is false and vicious. Such factors as accident, wear and tear, disease, and the hardening of arteries may bring about physical and/or mental impairment with no implication of guilt on the part of the victim. Nowhere is stereotype more vicious

than as in Jubilees, where the impairments of old
age are charged as consequences of guilt. It is a
proper thing to seek understanding of what may
have brought about impairment in an individual
case, but to generalize and moralize as does the book
of Jubilees is itself a sin against humanity.

Summary. Leviticus, then, has a strong requirement for the respect of age (19:32); and it preserves a
ruling based on age and sex distinctions which at
best is ambiguous as to implication and which opens
the way for age and sex discrimination as we read
into the passage what may or may not be there in its
intention (27:1-8). Once a figure like age 60—or 65 or
70 or whatever—enters into legislation, as here in
Leviticus, that number itself begins to gather its
own autonomy and to become a factor in shaping
attitudes, perspectives, and practices. It was not
overnight or strictly in a vacuum, for example, that
the retirement age in our time has been fixed at 65
or 70 years.

Numbers

As the title to this Bible book implies, numbering
the people of Israel, in particular the male population, was a big thing. A general census was taken,
and the males were classified by age for different
purposes, with special attention to military and religious service. The book offers some help as a witness
to ancient perspectives on age, and it can help as we
interact with it with a view to reassessing our own
perspectives on age.

The book begins with attention to a general census which focused on "every male, head by head,
from twenty years old and upward, all in Israel who
are able to go forth to war" (1:3,24,30, and else-

where). The book is preoccupied with Israel's over-
coming all threats from other nations and with her
ultimate taking of the land of Canaan, this involving
military battles with many nations. Obviously, 20
was considered the proper beginning age for military conscription. No terminal age is given, presumably a man being subject to military service so long
as able to serve. Nations throughout history have
had no reluctance to draft their young men for war,
and they have had no indisposition to utilize the
services of older men, although the "draft age" has
been limited. In Numbers, war was for men, as generally has been the case, with some exceptions in
ancient Israel and with the pattern now coming in
for reassessment.

A census for "the sons of Levi" included "every
male from a month old and upward" (3:14), this bearing upon the matter of their religious service and
inheritance rights. Yet another census was correlated with that of the sons of Levi: "Number all the
first-born males of the people of Israel, from a month
old and upward, taking their number by names"
(3:40). In the provision of cities, pasture rights, and
inheritance, the two numberings were important for
equitable decisions and settlements.

Age limits for Levites in active service are given
variously, with no certain way of resolving the differences. In Numbers 4:3,21,30, and elsewhere the
age for Levites is "from thirty years old up to fifty
years old." In Numbers 8:24 the Levites are "to perform the work in the service of the tent of meeting"
at the ages "from twenty-five years old and upward." But from the age of 50 their work is to be
modified, for "from the age of fifty years they shall
withdraw from the work of the service and serve no

more, but minister to their brethren in the tent of
meeting, to keep charge, and they shall do no service" (vv. 25-26). Apparently, the work was drasti-
cally modified but not altogether terminated. In 1
Chronicles 23:27 the Levites are numbered "from
twenty years old and upward," with no specified
terminal limit. One solution is to understand that the
ages did vary in practice, but this is not clear. A
Jewish explanation is that from 25 to 30 Levites
were initiated into lighter duties, that their main
function was from 30 to 50, and after 50 they per-
formed only light duties.[5] Snaith quotes Rabbi Hertz
to this effect: "A superannuated life need not be a
useless life."[6] One could hardly argue with this, but
what about a 50-year-old seeing himself or herself as
"superannuated"!

Whatever may be the answer to the seeming con-
fusion between the beginning ages of 25 and 30 for
Levites, there is solid tradition in Numbers for some
measure of retirement for Levites at age 50. A clue
is possible from chapter 4, where the duties of the
sons of Kohath, Gershon, and Merari (all sons of
Levi) are described in terms of "serving and bearing
burdens," with special attention to carrying the cur-
tains, frames, bars, pillars, bases, pegs, cords, and
other materials as the Tabernacle was moved from
place to place. This is manual labor. This is heavy
work, wagons used in part and shoulders used in
part (7:3,9). For such heavy work, it makes some
sense to have a terminal age, and 50 is one selection.
Obviously, some men are unsuited to carrying
heavy loads *before* 50, and some men can function
well *beyond* 50, but the idea of leaving such burden
to those best suited to it makes sense. As a "working
principle" an age limit can be serviceable; it is when

the working principle is turned into a law of nature or a divine law that it can become unjust, for this would be stereotype by which all 50-year-olds are seen to have the same health, competence, needs, and interests.

Most important is the seeming provision for "modified retirement" in 8:23-26. From the age of 50 the Levites were "to withdraw from the work of the service and serve no more" (v. 25). Were the instruction to end there, this would mean full retirement, but the sentence goes on, pointing to some form of continuing service: "but minister to their brethren in the tent of meeting, to keep the charge, and they shall do no service" (v. 26). This is not clear, but apparently at age 50 the Levites were to be relieved of some tasks but expected to continue in some form of ministry. Although not specified, possibly the burden of carrying the materials of the tabernacle (chapter 4) is what Levites were relieved of at age 50. If so, a significant principle is to be found here.

Whatever the particulars implied in 8:23-26, at the least there is provision for some form of modified retirement. Age 50 has nothing about it which makes it the necessary age for such modified retirement to begin. What is important is the recognition of the need of flexibility, both as to what is expected of a person in senior years (or any stage of life) and what particular age represents "seniority" for a given individual. Flexibility which is considerate of all concerned, those who serve and those whom they serve, seems to be the great principle which may be suggested to us by Numbers 8:23-26. The "all or nothing" principle is usually an unsound one, and it may be as inappropriate for "retirement" as anything else, especially when dictated and imposed at some arbitrary age which may not necessarily correspond to the needs or interests of those upon whom it is imposed.

Israel and the nations around her in the period covered by Numbers gave prominent place to older people. We have seen this already in our study of Leviticus. There are frequent references to "the elders" in Numbers; not only the elders of Israel (11:16,24-25,30; 16:25) but "the elders of Midian" and "the elders of Moab" (22:4,7). As seen above, it appears that making advantageous use of the experience of senior men in positions of power was widespread during the formative years of Israel. Cultures were not youth-oriented. If anything, they were more age-oriented. Apparently the "princes" sent on a crucial mission by Balak who were both numerous and "honorable" (22:15) were of the same status as "the elders" in Midian and Moab. When the nation's survival and well-being were at stake, these "elders" or "princes" were called upon for most responsible assignments.

When Moses found himself under heavy pressure on one occasion, he complained to God, "I am not able to carry all this people alone, the burden is too heavy for me" (11:14). In response, the Lord said to Moses, "Gather for me seventy men of the elders of Israel, whom you know to be the elders of the people and officers over them: and bring them to the tent of meeting, and let them take their stand with you" (v. 16). The elders were already a recognized group with some authority as "officers" among the people. What is reported as new here is the formation of a group of seventy elders to share some governing responsibility with Moses. These seventy elders may be the foundation to what is known later as the San-

hedrin, the highest court in Israel, presided over by
the high priest.

There are three strikingly similar stories in the
Law *(Torah)*, that is, the Pentateuch or first five
books of the Hebrew Bible, describing help given
Moses in governing the children of Israel (Ex.
18:13-27; Num. 11:10-17; Deut. 1:9-18). There are
both differences and close parallels, and just how
these three stories relate to one another is not an
easy problem.[7] What is important for our purpose is
the fact that three of the five books of the Law
describe the primary role in governance played by a
group of men called to the side of Moses. In Exodus,
following the counsel of Jethro, neither their number nor their age is specified, and they are not called
"elders." What was required was that they were
"able men . . . , such as fear God, men who are trust-
worthy and who hate a bribe" (Ex. 18:21). In Numbers the number seventy is specified, and they were
to be selected from an already existing group of
"elders of the people and officers over them" (Num.
11:16). Nothing is said as to their moral and personal
qualities; but if these seventy were drawn from
"elders" who are the same as appear in Exodus 18,
those qualities are already assumed. In Deuteronomy those chosen to bear the burden with Moses
were not numbered or called elders, but were to be
"wise, understanding, and experienced men" (Deut.
1:13). Whatever is to be made of the differences in
the stories, they all seem to point to the enlistment of
mature, experienced, good, and able people to carry
judicial and other governing responsibilities alongside Moses.

Summary. The book of Numbers emphasizes two
practices in ancient Israel which may inform and

guide us today in approach to the question of age: (1) the provision for a modified or flexible retirement, as in the case of the Levites, and (2) the utilization of "elders" in governance—men found able, just, honest, and such as fear God. No code, structure, or rule is foolproof or fail-safe; and certainly such is not to be lifted bodily out of the past and imposed upon a subsequent generation. That is not our suggestion. There are perspectives and principles found in Numbers which may inform and guide us today. Surely, for us today equal attention is to be given to all age groups and to women as well as men. The point is that in Numbers we see a serious attempt to tap the resources found in the "elders" and to provide deserved relief for those who have carried certain burdens their fair share of the time, as in the case of the Levites. Particular plans and procedures are matters for continuous reassessment and revision, and they are constantly to come under the discipline of other claims under which a community lives, individually and corporately.

Deuteronomy

Deuteronomy is not an easy book to understand, especially when attempt is made to see it in its historical context in terms of its harvesting of ancient traditions and shaping a theological stance for its own times. It would be far beyond the intention or scope of this book to undertake a critical review of the literature on the subject or assessment of the optional views of the origin, nature, and purpose of Deuteronomy. We do come to our study of Deuteronomic perspective on age only after having worked through the findings of at least some of the specialists in the field.

Centralization is clearly a major concern in Deuteronomy, whatever the immediate historical situation calling for such emphasis. Although the Passover was observed long before there was a Jewish Temple in Jerusalem, in Deuteronomy it is restricted to one designated place (Jerusalem): "You may not offer the passover sacrifice within any of your towns which the Lord your God gives you; but at the place which the Lord your God will choose, to make his name dwell in it, there you shall offer the passover sacrifice, in the evening at the going down of the sun, at the time you came out of Egypt" (16:5-6). Initially, the Passover had been celebrated in local family units, but in Deuteronomy it becomes a pilgrimage feast to be celebrated in only one common place as designated (which was Jerusalem).[8] Although something of the familial pattern was preserved, the Passover was affected by the strong centralization movement.

Deuteronomy also lays strong emphasis upon faithfulness to the one and only God and to the covenant made with him. With this are dire warnings against any concessions to the religions already in the land. Although scholars generally see the reflection of later conflicts and crises, Deuteronomy gives as its own setting the time of the death of Moses on the eve of the long-awaited entrance of the Israelites into the land of Canaan. Tension with Canaanite gods and religions is anticipated along with the problem of a seminomadic people now settling down in a nest of established cultures and religions. Against this background, Deuteronomy makes its call to rigid commitment to Israel's God and his laws, with a strong centralization included.

Now to come to our concern with perspectives on

age. It is most significant that to Deuteronomy the choosing of a king by Israel is permissible but treated as an almost indifferent matter (17:14-20).[9] The Israelites are told that if upon entering the land they want a king like the nations around them, they may have a king—but not a king like the kings around them. Severe limits are to be placed upon the king, if one is chosen. He must be of God's choosing, and he must not multiply for himself horses, wives, silver, and gold. Further, such a king must make for himself a copy of the book of the law which itself is under the authority of the Levitical priests, and the king must read this law daily and stay within its prescribed limits, so that he not only may "learn to fear the Lord his God" but "that his heart may not be lifted up above his brethren" (vv. 18-20).

With all its concern for centralization, Deuteronomy does not look to a king as the human authority to effect such centralization or to preserve the integrity of Israelite religion and life. The Levitical priests play a far greater role than envisioned for a king, if there is a king at all. Significantly, a major place is given in Deuteronomy to "the elders of the city in the gate" (22:15; see also 5:23; 19:12; 21:2-4,6,19-20; 22:15-18; 25:7-9; 27:1; 29:10; 31:9,28; 32:7). The elders are far more important to Deuteronomy than a possible king, not only mentioned many times more but assigned more responsible duties.

Deuteronomy sees the people of Israel not so much as a nation as a religious community, with a central place of worship and also with major structuring around "the elders of the city in the gate." In each town there were elders who sat at the gate of the town to function as judges (16:18; 21:19; 22:15). Law was not broken up into civil, criminal, religious, and other compartments; it was more unified, life being seen as of one piece. These elders/judges, then, had a most responsible role in the whole life of the people. There seems to be an equation of the terms judges, officers, and elders in the passages cited above.

Of the many examples in Deuteronomy of the role of "the elders of the city in the gate," some have to do with family relationships. The provision for the stoning of a stubborn son (21:18-21) strikes Christian conscience today with traumatic force, especially if Christian conscience gives place to the example and teachings of Jesus. Whatever we may be able to make of that—and certainly for the Christian the ultimate authority must rest with him who said, "But I say unto you" (Matt. 5:39,44)—there is here a significant implication for the role of elder persons in the life of the community. At least the disposition of the "stubborn and rebellious" son was not the exclusive right of the parents alone; final appeal was made to "the elders of his city at the gate of the place where he lives" (v. 19).[10] Parental responsibility and authority are recognized, but there is no place here for the idea that parents have such claim over their children that the community may be ignored. In a time of flagrant and frequent child abuse in the world today, especially in our own nation, this is a point to remember. There are limits to parental authority over their own children, and the community has its own responsibility in that relation. Deuteronomy makes much of this principle, and it recognizes the importance of "the elders" as ones in whom both wisdom and justice should be expected. To say the least, age here is respected and not despised.

Although Deuteronomy is decidedly favorable toward old age, it is not blind to the vulnerability of old

age to evil and to failure. It has no such doctrine as
that the old can do no wrong. In fact, its great hero
Moses himself is shown both in his greatness and in
his failure. Moses dominates the book, much of what
appears in the addresses and songs being ascribed to
Moses himself. Throughout the book, he is the un-
questioned leader of the children of Israel, not the
Levites, the elders, Joshua, or any other. Yet Moses
is depicted as fallible and faulty. In fact, the book
closes with the denial to Moses of the privilege of
entering the Promised Land. Those who talked
Aaron into making a golden calf for their worship
were denied the privilege of entering Canaan, but so
was Moses.

In its closing scene, Deuteronomy presents Moses
at 120 years of age and at full strength: "his eye was
not dim, nor his natural force abated" (34:7). He was
not denied entrance into the Promised Land or
further leadership of the children of Israel because
of being superannuated. He was not senile. He was
denied the privilege on the charge: "You broke faith
with me in the midst of the people of Israel at the
waters of Meribath-kadesh, in the wilderness of Zin,
because you did not revere me as holy in the midst of
the people of Israel" (32:51). Moses was "old" at the
time of his moral failure, but age is no guarantee that
one will do right even when he or she knows what is
right. Deuteronomy avoids the stereotype of equating old age with virtue or vice. Old and young alike
are capable of goodness and vulnerable to evil; and
Deuteronomy preserves its balance by its closing
picture of Moses in his failure (32:51) and Moses in
his greatness (34:10-12). There is no agism or stereotype here.

2
Age in the Historical Books

Old Testament scholars will recognize that the grouping in this chapter is somewhat arbitrary. In the Hebrew canon these writings fall partly in the second division, "The Prophets," and partly in the third section, "The Writings." We are following the order appearing in the English Bible, including books from Joshua through Nehemiah. Although basically historical in form and content, these writings are theological in concern. No one term adequately describes them, and the books grouped here are not homogeneous in character. The books will be studied individually, and the perspectives on age appearing in each book will be exhibited.

Joshua

The book of Joshua is concerned with Israel's conquest of her Promised Land, with special attention to Joshua as Moses' successor and to a lesser extent Caleb, Joshua's lifelong colleague in conquest. The book has relatively few direct references to age, but they are significant. Although the book recognizes that even so indomitable a man as Joshua must eventually "go the way of all the earth" when one is "old and well advanced in years" (23:2), age is viewed positively. There is not a hint of disrespect for the aged, and there is strong affirmation of the role of seniority in the life of the community.

The first mention of age in Joshua is nondiscriminating, where the destruction of Jericho is described as total: "Then they utterly destroyed all in the city, both men and women, young and old, oxen, sheep, and asses, with the edge of the sword" (6:21). In the perspective of the book, holy war is good and the extinction of the enemy is virtuous. Although not the intended point, war here does appear as that before which old and young alike suffer (as well as men and women, people and things). Of course, war is seen here as fought by "all the men of valor" (1:14), that is, those most able to fight. Apparently, the armies were made up for the most part of younger men, but they were led by older men, like Joshua and Caleb.

Seniority gets a strong affirmation in the book's portrayal of Caleb. At the age of 85 years he asked for the assignment of taking the difficult "hill country" with its "great fortified cities" (14:10-12). He was 40 when sent out by Moses from Kadesh-barnea to spy out the land, and now forty-five years later he could boast: "I am this day eighty-five years old. I am still as strong to this day as I was in the day that Moses sent me; my strength now is as my strength was then, for war, and for going and coming" (vv. 10-11).

Although age and aging are seen to lead to death, there is no "morbid" view of death as the inevitable to "all the earth" (23:14). That Joshua was "old and advanced in years" is faced as a matter of fact (13:1). Joshua's old age is not seen as disqualifying him, but it is seen as added reason for completing his task: "You are old and advanced in years, and there remains yet very much land to be possessed" (v. 1). Rather than resign, Joshua was to press on so as to leave the land occupied and properly divided up among the twelve tribes of Israel. Although "old and advanced in years," Joshua never appears as weak or deficient because of age. That his years were running out is faced openly and honestly, with no evasion or pretension that he would be an exception to the fact that death comes sooner or later to all people. Joshua was to run his course, do his job, and eventually leave ongoing responsibilities to his successors. In the book of Joshua, there is a positive view of life and death, of youth and age, each seen as normal and proper. Joshua is said to have died at 110 years, active until the end (24:29).

The role of older men in judging is explicit and recurrent in the book of Joshua. The "elders of Israel" shared responsibility with Joshua, standing with him in crises as when the Israelites faltered in faith or practice (7:6). In the conquest of Ai, Joshua went up "with the elders of Israel" (8:10), appearing with these elders both before the people of Israel and the people of Ai. Joshua thus found support in crises in these "elders." A special role for elders was found in judging cases among the people. Special provision was made through "cities of refuge" and through the wisdom of "the elders of the city" for the security of anyone who unintentionally took the life of another (20:1-9). These elders were senior adults, deemed best suited to fairness in judging such difficult cases. They held court "at the entrance of the gate of the city" (v. 4). In just such reliance upon "the elders of the city" may be found the model for the familiar senate governing of a nation. Although the custom eventually moved in the direction of including younger men in the senate, the original practice was to restrict the senate to seniors, as the word itself implies. A senator was an old man. *Se-nior* and *senator* both derive from a Latin word meaning old. So does the word *senile,* but when age is equated with senility those using the stereotype seem to forget that a senior or senator also is an age designation.

In two passages in Joshua, the age factor is linked with the highest governing authority in Israel: "Joshua summoned all Israel, their elders and heads, their judges and officers" (21:1; 24:1). The various offices or roles are not described here, but seniority is clearly a positive factor and in no way viewed negatively.

One closing note in Joshua is significant for the book's perspective on age: "And Israel served the Lord all the days of Joshua, and all the days of the elders who outlived Joshua and had known all the work which the Lord did for Israel" (24:31). Joshua is the unrivaled hero in the book, but "the elders" stood alongside him in the crises through which he led Israel; and Israel's fidelity to God after Joshua's death is credited to these elders. There is no denigration of youth in Joshua, and neither is there the "cult of youth" which denigrates age.

Judges

Judges is a strange book, with a certain cycle of conduct repeated throughout: the people of Israel forget their past and their God; they turn to pagan ways; they are abandoned to a fate of bondage to the pagans around them; they cry out for mercy and help; they are given a new leader and are restored to former privilege. Idolatry, murder, rape, vengeance, theft, and whatnot appear in story after story. No good case can be built here for young or old, men or

women, Israelites or pagans. The nearest approach
to the affirmation of any age group would favor the
oldsters, but nobody comes out well.

A key to an accounting for the vicious cycle may
be found in two observations: (1) "And the people
served the Lord all the days of Joshua, and all the
days of the elders who outlived Joshua, who had
seen all the work which the Lord had done for Israel" (2:7), and (2) "and there arose another generation after them who did not know the Lord or the
work which he had done for Israel" (2:10). The sta-
bility known under Joshua continued as long as "the
elders" contemporary with Joshua lived. The stabi-
lizing role of the elders, with Israel's failures following their loss, seems to be a deliberate theme in the
book of Judges.

A juxtaposition of youth and old age occurs in
8:13-17, with youth suffering by comparison.
Whether so intended may be debated. As the story
stands, "a young man of Succoth" betrayed "the
officers and elders of Succoth, seventy-seven men"
by writing down their names and exposing them to
arrest and execution. From the perspective of Succoth, the young man must have been a traitor and
the elders the victims. Of course, the man to whom
the elders of Succoth were delivered was Gideon, so
the story may intend to glorify the young man. In
any event, in the story the youth betrays his fellow
townsmen, and the elders are betrayed by the youth.

Bias does appear in the stereotype of youth, where
Gideon's firstborn son Jether failed to slay his
father's enemies at his father's command, thus
explained: "But the youth did not draw his sword;
for he was afraid, because he was still a youth"
(8:20). The precise age of the "men of valor" (see also

6:12) is not indicated, but it is likely that the armies glorified in Judges included young men. For all this, the one explicit charge of being afraid is explained in terms of being young. On the other hand, although the hero Gideon's age is not specified at the outset of his role as deliverer of Israel, his many triumphs in battle seem to continue until his death "in a good old age" (8:32). How old Gideon was at death is not disclosed, but he lived long enough to have had "seventy sons, his own offspring, for he had many wives" (v. 30).

In the story of "a young Levite," a priest, youth again comes out in bad light in the book of Judges (17:1 to 18:31). In the story, "a young man of Bethlehem in Judah, of the family of Judah, who was a Levite" set out to find some place to live. He found his way to the home of Micah in Ephraim and hired out as Micah's priest (18:4). Micah's own character may be inferred from his having stolen silver from his own mother, later returning it and getting it back in order to make of it "a graven image and a molten image" to go along with his shrine and other religious trappings (17:1-6). Not only did this young Levite hire out for such service, but later he switched his service to some Danites who offered him more (18:19-20). In the story, old and young alike seem to be engaged in idolatry and attempted manipulation of God; but the one person who sells himself to the highest offer is throughout the story identified as "a young man." Added to the story of "the young man of Succoth" (8:13-17), the book of Judges may intend to take a low view of youth. However, there is more to be observed.

In chapter 11 "the elders of Gilead" (vv. 8-11) are featured, and they are presented as defenders of Israel against the Ammonites. Needing a leader, they turned to Jephthah the Gileadite, a mighty warrior (11:1). That they picked a winner is clear. Their picking such a man as Jephthah may reflect maturity and grace in the elders or just indifference to qualities other than gifts of leadership in warfare. Jephthah was a "son of a harlot" (v. 1), and he was rejected by his father's family, cast out with nothing. Not holding Jephthah responsible for his heritage could speak well for the maturity and fairness of "the elders of Gilead." But Jephthah is pictured not only as the passive victim of his family background; he is pictured as on his own having engaged in a less than commendable vocation: "and worthless fellows collected round Jephthah, and went raiding with him" (v. 3). However all this reflects on "the elders," this was their man. That they enlisted Jephthah with a view to mending his ways is less attested in the story than that they simply sought him out as a winner. Age does not come out too well here. At least its "bill of health" is not completely laundered.

The book of Judges closes with a long and involved story which includes among others "an old man" (19:16-22) and "the elders of the congregation" (21:16). Again, nobody comes out well by Christian standards. The "old man" first appears happily in the role of generous host, opening his home to a stranger and the stranger's concubine. Another side of the old man is seen when during the night some "base fellows" of the city pounded on his door and demanded that the host surrender his male guest to them, "that we may know him," apparently with homosexual intent (19:22). The old man, the master of the house, explained to the mob that he could not

comply with their request, for what they proposed
was wicked and vile (v. 23). Instead, he volunteered
his own virgin daughter and the concubine that the
base fellows might ravish them and do with them
whatever they wished (v. 24). When the mob rejected this offer, the guest thrust out his concubine,
and the base men so ravished her through the night
that she was found dead on the doorstep the next
morning. A long story of vengeance follows, with
"the elders of the congregation" (21:16) devising a
strategy for kidnapping foreign virgins to replenish
the depleted stock in Benjamin, following the family
feud between Israelites and Benjamites over the
slaying of the concubine.

We must conclude where we began. In the book of
Judges, neither youth nor age, men nor women,
Israelites nor "pagans," come out well. At best, the
picture is mixed. Fortunately, better models appear
elsewhere in the Old Testament.

Ruth

This four-chapter book features throughout the
young woman for whom the book is named (4:12),
portraying her as a model in devotion and loyalty to
her widowed mother-in-law, Naomi. In the book
there is considerable implication for age/youth relationships, especially with regard to "the generation
gap."

Although Boaz, seemingly an older man, and
Ruth, a "young woman" (4:12), form a beautiful relationship seemingly beyond the reach of any rival
suitor, at least the awareness of the "generation
gap" is reflected. Boaz senses a possible threat from
the younger generation, and he "charged the young
men" who worked in his fields and into which Ruth

had gone to glean "not to molest" her (2:9). Boaz
further reflected his sense of the generation gap
when he commended Ruth for her great kindness in
giving herself to him instead of going after "young
men, whether poor or rich" (3:10). The story is told
with an awareness of the threat age can feel in the
presence of youth. Boaz seems definitely to sense
such a threat. His strong position as belonging to the
"landed gentry" does not entirely free him of a sense
of vulnerability if he must compete with younger
men. Whether such fear is justified or not, it is real.
Boaz does not stand alone in his sense of vulnerability to "the younger generation." Any informed concern for older people must understand factors and
fears which were concerns to even so privileged and
"secure" a man as Boaz.

Naomi's concern that Ruth not go into the field of
some other but that she go out with the maidens of
Boaz is likewise attributed explicitly to her fear that
otherwise Ruth might be "molested" (2:22). Probably Naomi's real concern was that Ruth come to the
attention of Boaz as the best option for Ruth, but in
the story is clearly the assumption on Naomi's part
that any unattached woman is vulnerable to strange
men, whatever their age. For Naomi, then, the issue
was the vulnerability of any young woman to men;
for Boaz it was the threat of youth to age, at least in
competing for a woman's love. Of course, neither
sex nor age group has a monopoly on molesting or
not molesting other people.

A more positive coping with the "generation gap"
is reflected in the beautiful relationship between the
widowed Naomi and her two widowed daughters-in-
law, Orpah and Ruth. Naomi could have imposed
maximum pressure upon Orpah and Ruth to make

their widowed mother-in-law their top priority. Instead, the older woman gave priority to the younger
women, releasing them from any obligation to herself and encouraging them to return to their native
land of Moab and each to her mother's house (1:8).
She went beyond this in her concern that they build
for themselves a new life: "May the Lord deal kindly
with you, as you have dealt kindly with the dead and
with me. The Lord grant that you may find a home,
each of you in the house of her husband!" (vv. 8-9).
Here is a model of wisdom and concern on the part of
the older for the younger generation.

On the side of Orpah and Ruth, the transcendence
of "the generation gap" was equally successful. The
younger women were as considerate of the older
woman as Naomi was for them. Both insisted upon
remaining with Naomi, putting concern for her
above any self-serving course. Eventually, Orpah
and Ruth opted for different courses, Orpah leaving
her mother-in-law and Ruth remaining with her, but
both acted in full accord with Naomi. Orpah yielded
to Naomi's judgment as to what was best for Orpah;
Ruth remained firm in her commitment to remain
with Naomi. Different courses were taken, but the
story implies that both Orpah and Ruth acted out of
deepest devotion to Naomi. Whatever difference in
evaluating options, the story is firm in its portrayal
of the mutual love and commitment which transcended the generation gap. This is no "book of
rules" for what to do in a difficult situation between
two generations, but it is a model as to the mutual
love and concern which should govern the exercise
of the options at hand.

The "elders of the city" play an important role in
the book as witnesses and guarantors of justice, as

Boaz appealed to them in his negotiations for clear-
ing with all concerned as he sought to acquire Ruth
as his wife (4:2,4,9,11). This simply reflects the fact
that communities did look to age for wisdom and justice. Unfortunately, "the elders" did not always justify the confidence placed in them.

The book closes with a clear recognition of the
dependence of the aged upon their children and/or
grandchildren. When a son was born to Boaz and
Ruth, this brought a special joy to "the women"
around Naomi, and they said to her, "Blessed be the
Lord, who has not left you this day without next of
kin, and may his name be renowned in Israel! He
shall be to you a restorer of life and a nourisher of
your old age; for your daughter-in-law who loves
you, who is more to you than seven sons, has borne
him" (4:14-15). In the perspective here, it is assumed
that the young will provide for the needs of such a
one as Naomi in her old age. Again, this is no "rule
book" for universal application; but it does uncover
a positive factor implying not a "generation gap"
but rather "generation bonds." Sometimes the dependence of children upon their parents gives way
to the dependence of parents upon their children.
Who is dependent upon whom is a matter of circum-
stance; that bonds and not gap govern the relationship is a matter of love and authentic personhood.

In summary, the book of Ruth may stereotype
young men, seeing them as a threat, whether to
young women or old men or both. Apart from this,
there is no trace of negativity toward youth. There
clearly is no negativity toward older people. The
book is positive toward both Naomi and Boaz; and
though the age of neither is explicit, both are seen as
at least in "the older generation." Of course, Ruth is

the central figure in the story; and she is both
"young" (4:12) and esteemed throughout. The book
is especially rewarding for an in-depth study of "the
generation gap."

First Samuel

Several interesting persons appear in 1 Samuel:
Hannah; her son, Samuel; Eli, the priest; Saul, the
first king of Israel; David, his designated successor;
and Jonathan, son of Saul and David's closest friend.
Eli was "very old" (2:22), with wayward sons and
the warning that his family line would be cut off, put
bluntly: "There shall not be an old man in your
house forever" (2:31-32). Samuel was "a prophet of
the Lord" (3:20), the real successor to Eli. For all his
disappointments and frustrations, the priest Eli remained active until he was "ninety-eight years old,"
even though virtually blind by that time (4:15). He
was still active as a judge at the city gate when he
died: "Eli fell over backward from his seat by the
side of the gate; and his neck was broken and he
died, for he was an old man and heavy" (4:18). Samuel, too, continued until he "became old" (8:1); and
like Eli he was followed by wayward sons, his sons
becoming judges who "took bribes and perverted
justice" (8:3). This breakdown in the line of Eli and
Samuel prompted "the elders of Israel" to call upon
Samuel to provide for Israel a king to govern them.

Most of the book centers around Saul and David
and is instructive for our purpose at two points at
least: (1) factors leading to a miserable old age and (2)
the tensions of the generation gap. For all the promise of Saul's youth, his later years were decadent
ones. A major factor in Saul's self-destruction was

his deep fear of David, whom he saw only as a threat to his throne.

Any notion that old age is necessarily one of beauty and strength is refuted by the story of Saul. His seemingly best years were those of his youth. He first appears in the story as "a handsome young man," head and shoulders above everyone else (9:2). As a young man he seemed open to God, a man "also among the prophets" (10:11). When sought out for his coronation as king, his modesty was such that he was found having "hidden himself among the baggage" (10:22). Saul became increasingly self-centered and self-serving; and he became increasingly suspicious of those around him, fearful for his position, and especially fearful of David, his son-in-law and heir apparent. His fear became madness. Finally, his whole world caved in around him; and he took his life by falling upon his own sword (31:4).

Saul felt threatened by David and became increasingly psychotic. He developed a love/hate relationship toward David (16:21). He had a low self-image: "little in your own eyes" (15:17). He indulged in self-pity. He craved pity and apparently felt sorry for himself (22:8). He never learned to control his anger (11:6; 18:8,10). He embittered himself with the lust for vengeance (14:24). He became increasingly neurotic (16:14-23; 18:10-11; 19:9). He feared that he would be "cut off" and that his name would be lost (24:21). Of course, David's appointment as Saul's successor during the lifetime of Saul was the focal point in the tension, even though David sought variously to demonstrate his loyalty to Saul. It was not enough comfort to Saul to be assured that David would only succeed him, not displace him. Saul was

unwilling to see David in his place. Here was an old
man unable or unwilling to come to terms with his
own limitations, including the finitude of his own life
and reign. Trying to deny the inevitable, he has-
tened it. For Saul the generation gap was real, and
he could never cope with it. To Saul, David was the
"young man" (17:58) who represented the major
threat to all that life meant to him.

Saul's empty and miserable old age did not just
happen. Throughout the book is traced the sowing
of seeds which yielded the miserable harvest. Saul
finally confessed, "I have played the fool" (26:21).
He had done just that. One who appeared to be a
modest, wholesome, and trusting young man became increasingly a selfish, self-serving, self-trust-
ing older man. In trying to save himself, he destroyed himself. Years before he took his own life
upon his own sword, he destroyed himself by his
ambitions and fears. If we are to learn from Saul, we
should see that what we are in the older years probably is what we were becoming in earlier years. We
may also find evidence of what the "generation gap"
can do to us, or at least what we take to be a generation gap. To understand Saul, we must understand
that youth can be a threat to old age, whether youth
so intends it or not. Although there is no necessary
conflict between age and youth, it is not uncommon
for age to see it as such. Saul's old age could have
been radically different had he been less afraid of
being "cut off" and more concerned that young
David have his chance to be. There was room for
Saul and David, but Saul found it increasingly difficult to believe this to be so.

From 1 Samuel we may learn not only of one's
power to self-destruct, as in the case of Saul. We

may learn of one's need of compassion (23:21). We may learn of the community's responsibility to be understanding of and helpful to the older person who feels threatened by the younger, with or without due cause. We may learn that neither side can solve the problem alone. Whatever David's sensitivity to Saul, Saul may yet self-destruct. This is most likely if the younger Saul does not in early years sow the seed yielding a happy harvest.

Second Samuel

Except for one story (19:31-40), 2 Samuel has little to offer on the subject of age. That one story, however, offers a rewarding study of an 80-year-old man, Barzillai. Out of his resources Barzillai had given support to the beleaguered David during Absalom's revolt against his father; and now David offers to reward Barzillai by taking him along in his return to power. The story features Barzillai's tactful decline of the reward, protecting his own independence and integrity without affront to his king.

The writer of 2 Samuel saw Barzillai as "a very aged man, eighty years old" (19:32). On the surface, Barzillai seems to have seen himself at age 80 to have little left to live for except to await his death and burial in his own city near the grave of his father and mother (v. 37). He reflects no regrets, fears, or apprehensions, seeing his anticipated death as that to which life moves normally. In declining David's invitation to join the king's party, Barzillai appears to view life beyond 80 as rather meaningless: "I am this day eighty years old; can I discern what is pleasant or what is not? Can your servant taste what he eats or what he drinks? Can I still listen to the voice of singing men and singing women?

Why then should your servant be an added burden to my lord the king?" (v. 35).

Taken at face value, this is a low view of life beyond 80. It assumes that life ends at 80, a view not shared generally in the Old Testament. In fact, this is our first encounter with so negative a view of old age, where even the taste buds fail and one at 80 cannot distinguish between what is pleasant and what is not. Worst of all is the assumption that the presence of an 80-year-old would be an "added burden" to those around him. This is a part of the familiar perspective which equates old age with burden to family and/or society, age thus viewed as a problem and not a challenge. There is nothing about age 80 which so divides meaningful life from meaningless life, and such perspective is not supported generally in Jewish literature. If Barzillai really felt this way about himself, he needed all the affirmation he could get. There are old people who thus see themselves, and they need help.

It is possible that Barzillai's self-depreciating words are to be understood in a more positive sense. His disposition seems actually to have been to render service to his king without expectation or desire for reward. When David responds with equal generosity, Barzillai so responded as to preserve his own integrity and dignity without the appearance of ingratitude to his king. He declined the reward by representing himself as unsuited to it. His very speech reflects a poised person, far from decrepit or decadent. He does not talk like a defeated old man. He is master of the situation, offering service without reward and giving his king freedom to go on without him. Unlike Saul, Barzillai has accepted the inevitability of death, and he is prepared to accept it when it comes. In sum, although Barzillai outwardly plays down his powers, he functions as a man in full possession of his wits and in charge of his own life, even able tactfully to keep his beloved king from taking over his life and managing it. At age 80, Barzillai was able to work around his king's strategy and keep control of his own life. The deeper the story is probed, the more positive is the picture which emerges of this "very aged man, eighty years old."

One further point may be made. Barzillai clearly preferred to spend his remaining days at home, in his own city and where his parents were buried. He preferred home to David's palace. Most older people cling to the familiar surroundings of home and to the management of their own lives, if possible to the very end. This is something which family and society may well remember. Some older persons cannot take care of themselves and should be cared for otherwise. However, where at all viable, Barzillai speaks for legions, not just for himself. Other factors must often be considered, but let us never forget the extreme importance to Barzillai and his counterparts of the peace of mind, satisfaction, and fulfillment which may come from just being able to live out one's life "at home."

First Kings

Any naive equating of age with virtue gets a setback in 1 Kings. There is no intended denigration of age. In fact, there is no intention of glorifying or denigrating youth or age in this book; but in the tracing of many lives, chiefly royal, nobody comes out clean. From beginning to end, the book is about human failure, with few positive notes. Probably the principle best attested is that in old age one tends to

reflect qualities latent from youth. Put otherwise, it
is in one's younger years that the basic choices are
made determining the quality of the later ones. People do not just happen to turn out to be ugly old people or beautiful old people. There is some correlation
between one's youth and one's age. On the other
hand, as seen earlier, a "Jacob" can become an "Israel." In 1 Kings, unfortunately, the "Jacobs" simply become more "Jacoby."

The book begins with David in his last days, and
they are less than beautiful: "Now David was old and
advanced in years" (1:1), and he saw himself as
"about to go the way of all the earth" (2:2). Although
no more than 70 years of age (2 Sam. 5:4), David was
physically depleted. In his last illness, when cover-
ing failed to get him warm, there was resort to
David's lifelong passion—women. His attendants
searched the land for "a beautiful maiden" to be the
bed-partner of the old king, but even this attempt at
sexual arousal failed (1:4). It is a commentary on age-
group perspectives that "a beautiful maiden" could
be requisitioned for the supposed sexual/health
needs of an old man. Interestingly, there is no story
of a handsome young man being conscripted to
warm the bed of a dying old woman.

When the dying king's son Adonijah tried to
usurp his father's throne (1:5-10), it was not so much
a matter of a "generation gap" as a power struggle
between brothers, Adonijah and Solomon (1:11-14).
True, Adonijah did not even await his father's death
before claiming the throne, itself a disrespect of
youth for age; but the overriding motive was to beat
Solomon to the punch, grabbing the throne before
his brother could get it. Only secondarily does this

sordid story reflect the tensions of the generation gap.

Solomon is a clear illustration that length of days is no assurance of improvement. When one is going the wrong direction, it does not help to speed up. Solomon, like Saul, shows up better in youth than in old age, even though his "old age" probably did not exceed 60 years. He appears best when as a young king he asked for wisdom to discern good and evil, prizing that above wealth, honor, or long life: "Give thy servant therefore an understanding mind to govern thy people, that I may discern between good and evil; for who is able to govern this thy great people?" (3:9). God commended Solomon: "Because you have asked this, and have not asked for yourself long life or riches or the life of your enemies, but have asked for yourself understanding to discern what is right, behold I now do according to your word" (3:10-12).

Despite this excellent beginning, Solomon failed precisely where he should have been most concerned not to fail. He practiced vengeance (2:28-35), enslaved men (9:15,21), exploited women (11:3), served heathen gods (11:4), and in various other ways documented through his own waywardness his concession, "for there is no man who does not sin" (8:46). This is not to overlook positive factors in the life of Solomon. It is to be observed that 1 Kings adds to the beautiful introduction of Solomon in his request for "an understanding mind ... to discern between good and evil" (3:9) the sad sequel: "He had seven hundred wives, princesses, and three hundred concubines; and his wives turned away his heart. For when Solomon was old his wives turned away his heart after other gods; and his heart was not true to the Lord his God, as was the heart of David his father" (11:3-4). Aging should be a factor on the side of goodness, but with Solomon it was not.

The elders in 1 Kings proved to be capable of virtue or vice. In the story of Rehoboam (12:6-15) "the old men" show up well and "the young men" poorly. The old men gave Rehoboam, son of Solomon, some mature and wise advice, that he deal respectfully with the people: "If you will be a servant to this people today and serve them, and speak good words to them when you answer them, then they will be your servants for ever" (v. 7). The young men gave the opposite counsel, that Rehoboam outdo his father in laying upon the people a heavy yoke and that he chastise them not with whips but with scorpions (vv. 10-11). The results were predictable, and the policies of the young men led to chaos.

Lest age be stereotyped as wise and kind, and youth as foolish and cruel, 1 Kings must be heard further. In the story of King Ahab and Naboth's vineyard (21:1-24) "the elders and the nobles who dwelt in the city" proved to be no more than weak stooges in the hands of a cruel Jezebel (vv. 8-14). Following Jezebel's orchestration of a "trial," these "elders" and "nobles" simply rubber-stamped Jezebel's demand that Naboth be killed. Jezebel got her way; Ahab got an innocent man's vineyard; and "the elders and the nobles" expedited the scheme. The old men who counseled Rehoboam were wise and good; the elders who served Jezebel and Ahab were weak and crooked. There is no one-to-one relationship between age and goodness, even though aging should favor goodness.

Second Kings

The most striking passage in 2 Kings bearing on the question of age involves the prophet Elisha and at least forty-two boys (2:23-25). Here is the "generation gap" erupting with a vengeance. The story is one of youth's contempt for age and the merciless retaliation of age against youth. The story is that of an incident on the road from Jericho to Bethel, quite unlike a story Jesus told about an incident on the road from Jerusalem to Jericho (Luke 10:25-37).

In the story, as Elisha was going up to Bethel, "some small boys came out of the city and jeered at him, saying, 'Go up, you baldhead! Go up, you baldhead!'" (v. 23). Elisha turned, saw the boys, cursed them in the name of the Lord, "And two she-bears came out of the woods and tore forty-two of the boys" (v. 24).

On one side of the generation gap is the taunting of age by youth. Elisha is reduced to a baldhead. There is no known research which can demonstrate whether children have learned this "reductionism" from adults or adults from children. Both practice it to this day. It was no isolated, childish game to taunt an old man about his bald head. It is not uncommon today for culture's finest to reduce a human being to a baldhead. Children can be insensitive to the feelings of older people as they joke about a mark of age (though baldness comes quite early to many); but the insensitivity is not limited to children, nor is it limited to baldness. These "small boys" were not cute; they were cruel. Where they learned it is not disclosed.

But what about the other side of the generation

gap? Elisha blew his cool and cursed these little boys
"in the name of the Lord" (v. 24). Being "chewed
out" by a prophet and "chewed up" by two she-
bears is rather severe punishment for misbehavior
of "some small boys." More than an isolated event
may be implied. In any event, the "gap" here was a
"Grand Canyon." There was shouting on both sides,
but there was not communication. The very violence
into which the incident erupted is warning as to how
deep and wide the chasm can become between youth
and age. It is occasion for reassessment of the relationship between youth and age, with a view to better understanding on the part of each for the other.
Parents and all adults must reckon with the growing
problem of child abuse today. Children and all young
people must reckon with the problem of the abuse of
older people, whether it occurs through the brutality of tongue or weapons otherwise.

It may be more than coincidence that the story of
the clash between the prophet and the boys is told in
a book which makes several references to human
sacrifice, where parents actually sacrificed their
children to their gods (16:3; 17:17; 23:10). Of course,
Elisha would have no tolerance for such heathen
practice. This heathen practice did occur around
Israel, and it penetrated even Israelitish practice. It
was "in the air." There was in certain religious piety
such an extreme as child sacrifice as a part of
"piety." Religion, certainly that of Jesus Christ,
offers to the parent/child and the adult/youth relationship the highest redemptive quality. Religion
(almost anything passes under this label) can "sanctify" the ultimate in the dehumanizing of parent and
child, adult and youth. Ancient and modern practice

may well come under the judgment and redemption
ready at hand for us in Jesus of Nazareth.

In 2 Kings is embedded a principle from "the book
of the law of Moses" which reads: "The fathers shall
not be put to death for the children, or the children
be put to death for the fathers, but every man shall
die for his own sin" (14:6). The principle is applied in
this context only to an ancient problem of idol worship; but the principle of equity between children
and parents — youth and age — is basic and far-reach-
ing. Whatever else it implies, it recognizes the rights
as well as the responsibilities of the individual. The
right to be, to be oneself, is a basic right of our
humanity. Age has the right to be. Youth has the
right to be. Rights imply responsibility, the responsible exercise of rights, whether by older people like
Elisha or younger people like the small boys who
jeered him.

First Chronicles

Aging makes inevitable "the changing of command," "the passing of the torch," or however the
succession of persons or generations is expressed.
First Chronicles contains an excellent case study in
such succession, in several closely related passages
in which David "puts the record straight" as to his
part and his son Solomon's in the building of the
Temple at Jerusalem (chaps. 22—29). David knows
that the actual building of the Temple will fall to
Solomon, but he goes to great lengths repeatedly to
explain how he made all the necessary plans for the
Temple and gathered the materials and skilled work-
men for the project. He wants the record to show
that his great experience anticipated the immaturity

of his son and made all the hard decisions and preparations for him in advance. Obviously, the old man,
for all the grace with which he relates to Solomon,
finds it hard to turn loose the reins to his son, and he
wants to make secure the credit due himself.

Retirement can be a trauma. Turning loose to
one's children or younger persons can be a crisis
experience. As for David, so it is for multitudes
today. First Chronicles gives us a good case study
for understanding the problem to older people when
the time comes to give way to a younger person. It
offers a good case study for any of us who would prepare for this inevitable passage in life. Whether
David's feelings, concerns, and behavior are seen as
proper or improper, they are real. The first step in
relating supportively or redemptively to an older
person struggling, like David, with "retirement" or
"succession" is understanding. Family and community need to understand what it is like to be in
David's situation. Older people need a clear understanding of themselves in this situation.

David's deep feelings are hardly concealed in his
careful explanations of his role in paving the way for
his son Solomon, providing for his son almost a "fail-
safe" anticipation of his needs. Feelings are almost
transparent in David's explanation: "Solomon my
son is young and inexperienced, and the house that
is to be built for the Lord must be exceedingly mag-
nificent, of fame and glory throughout all lands; I
will therefore make preparation for it" (22:5). In a
long, detailed account, David's elaborate collecting
of materials and enlistment of skilled personnel is
given. David does not neglect to lecture Solomon as
to his proper part, reminding Solomon that he will
enjoy a period of "rest," following David's years of

bringing the nation to its prosperity and security from its enemies. It was "with great pains" (22:14) that David made such elaborate preparations, and he saw to it that Solomon was adequately briefed as to his role. Thus David provided for and lectured Solomon when "David was old and full of days" (23:1).

Not only did David lecture Solomon as to every detail of "the plan" for the Temple, but he lectured the assembly as to how it was to be supportive of his son: "Solomon my son, whom alone God has chosen, is young and inexperienced, and the work is great; for the palace will not be for man but for the Lord God. So I have provided for the house of my God, so far as I was able" (29:1-2*a*). There follows another recital of all that David has accomplished, providing for Solomon all that he will need: plans, materials, personnel. Of course, David explained that he and his people were able to make such generous provision only because it all really belonged to the Lord (29:14). Lest anyone may have missed the point, David made it once more: "Grant to Solomon my son that with a whole heart he may keep thy commandments, thy testimonies, and thy statutes, performing all, and that he may build the palace *for which I have made provision*" (29:19, italics added).

First Chronicles closes with the final "change of command." After forty years as king, David "died in a good old age, full of days, riches and honor; and Solomon his son reigned in his stead" (29:28). David saw the inevitable as it drew near, and he faced it with courage and grace. Nonetheless, it is apparent that the transition for David was not easy. He reached out for understanding and appreciation. His concern for Solomon's "youth and inexperience" could be taken as patronizing; and his lavish provision for Solomon's needs could appear as preempting Solomon's own role or reducing it to that of a construction foreman. However understood or assessed, 1 Chronicles does offer an intriguing case study in the problems which obtain even where a relationship between father and son was as positive as that of David and Solomon. The "Davids" when "old and full of days" need to be understood. They need help in understanding themselves and accepting themselves. They need help in understanding the "Solomons." The first step in understanding is the recognition that there are feelings, fears, anxieties, and concerns in every "David" and in every "Solomon" among us. Those of us with little expertise in such understanding of personhood can compensate with a lot of love and some real effort. Around us are people with expertise to help us all with problems of "retirement," "the changing of command," or "the passing of the torch."

Second Chronicles

Nothing new on the subject of age appears in 2 Chronicles, but there is some reinforcement to perspectives already encountered. The story of Rehoboam's unfortunate rejection of the counsel of "the old men" in favor of that of "the young men" is repeated (10:6-19; see also 1 Kings 12:1-20). In 2 Chronicles, as in 1 Kings, the old men counsel King Rehoboam to deal kindly with the nation, in the confidence that such approach would bring out the best in people; whereas the young men counseled the king to be much harsher than his father Solomon had been. In both books, the immature and harsh disposition of the young men proves counterproductive. The writers clearly recognize the superior wisdom of the old men.

To recognize with 2 Chronicles, as with the parallel in 1 Kings, that age should be on the side of wisdom is itself a matter of wisdom. However, to assume that all young men are immature and rash and that all old men are mature and wise does not follow. Aging should favor one in both wisdom and spirit, but whether it does so or not depends upon the basic direction of a life. If one is going the wrong way, the passing years simply worsen the condition. If one is open to truth and right, aging should be an advantage. What is clear from 2 Chronicles, as with 1 Kings, is that age is seen as on the side of wisdom.

A further evidence of perspective in 2 Chronicles appears in the story of the struggle between Rehoboam and Jeroboam, a servant of Solomon who defied Rehoboam. Rehoboam's disadvantage is ascribed to his youth, the attack by Jeroboam and his supporters coming "when Rehoboam was young and irresolute and could not withstand them" (13:7). Stereotype may be seen in the linking of timidity with youth, for many young people are quite bold. In any event, 2 Chronicles again sees age as advantage and youth as disadvantage in governing other people. Of course, the advantage of age may be lost, and the disadvantage of youth may be overcome.

Once more in 2 Chronicles, age is seen positively in the case of Jehoiada: "But Jehoiada grew old and full of days, and died; he was a hundred and thirty years old at his death" (24:15). Jehoiada's old age is not explicitly credited to his goodness, but the two are at least juxtaposed: "And they buried him in the city of David among the kings, because he had done good in Israel, and toward God and his house" (24:16). Not length of years but burial among the kings in the city of David is the reward of his goodness. That Jehoiada "grew old and full of days" is seen positively. Not to be overlooked is the realism behind the simple statement, "and died." The Old Testament never hedges on the matter of death. It generally esteems old age, but its realism never obscures the fact that all die. However many the years, 130 for Jehoiada, they lead inevitably to death. Neither youth nor age can be healthy if the fact of death is not included in one's affirmation of self. There is a morbid and defeatist way to look at death, and there is an honest and triumphant way of looking at it. Second Chronicles is honest and triumphant in saying, "But Jehoiada grew old and full of days, and died."

As the text stands (see 2 Kings 24:8), the comment on Jehoiachin is remarkable: "Jehoiachin was eight years old when he began to reign, and he reigned three months and ten days in Jerusalem. He did what was evil in the sight of the Lord" (36:9). He apparently was some mean kid![1] The refrain "and he did what was evil in the sight of the Lord" appears throughout these chronicles for kings young and old, implying that character and conduct are not determined by the age factor alone.

Ezra

A new note is struck in Ezra in the recognition of responsible assignment to young men alongside older ones: "They appointed the Levites, from twenty years old and upward, to have the oversight of the work of the house of the Lord" (3:8b). This had to do with the rebuilding of the Temple in Jerusalem at the return of the exiles from Babylon. That the significant group of Levites included 20-year-olds is itself significant. That they were included among the overseers in the rebuilding of the Temple is likewise significant. There is no hint here that youth is deficient in any of the qualities expected of the Levites. The particular work here was building construction; but not to be overlooked is that at age 20, one could be a Levite, whose chief ministry was in the Temple services, not building construction.

No agism may be derived from the report that some of the "old men" wept when they saw how far short the reconstructed Temple fell by comparison with that built under Solomon, while other "old men" shouted with joy. Some old men lived in the past and could not rejoice in the newly built Temple. Other old men lived in their present, and they rejoiced in what they had. Old age is found here in both patterns, some imprisoned by the past and some celebrating life as they met it. Age itself does not determine the perspective or mood, and it is stereotype to say that it does. Individuality, whether young or old, can be the determining force in perspective or attitude.

The role of "the elders" is prominent in Ezra, explicitly with reference to the rebuilding of the Temple (5:5,9; 6:7-14) and with reference to discipline within the community (10:8,14). It is not clear to what extent "calendar age" figured in one's being included among "the elders." As already seen, at the outset "the elders" were senior men, but gradually the office came to be less tied to age (as is the case with "senators").

Nehemiah

There is nothing in this book bearing directly on the subject of age, and it is precarious to derive much even by implication. The book is concerned with the rebuilding of the wall around Jerusalem. Although the focus is upon a literal wall, the book is also concerned with such "walls" as sabbath observance, ritual acts, and avoidance of "foreign women" as wives, thus seeking to keep the Jews clean and pure. Prominence is given to "the priests, the nobles, the officials" (2:16) and to "the prophets" and at least one "prophetess" (6:14), but the age factor is not explicit. A patriarchal pattern is assumed throughout, with frequent mention of "the heads of fathers' houses" (8:13) or simply "our fathers" (9:9).

Some priority for age is implied in the ordering of the community; but age is not seen as itself assuring the quality of life. The "fathers" can be esteemed, but they likewise can be censured: "But they [the Egyptians?] and our fathers acted presumptuously and stiffened their neck and did not obey thy commandments; they refused to obey, and were not mindful of the wonders which thou didst perform among them; but they stiffened their neck and appointed a leader to return to their bondage in Egypt" (9:16-17). Again, age should be on the side of goodness, but there is no necessary one-to-one relationship between age and quality of life.

3
Age in the Wisdom Books

Again, grouping follows the order of the English Bible and is somewhat arbitrary. Esther is not one of the "wisdom books," but it does belong with these others to "The Writings" in the Hebrew canon. Also, "the Writings" in the Hebrew canon include various other books. Most of the writings surveyed in this chapter are poetic and belong to the Wisdom Literature. The varied perspectives on age will be examined book by book.

Esther

This is an unusual book, even though to Christians one of the most familiar of all Old Testament writings. It is significant to Judaism chiefly because it provides a historical base for the Feast of Purim. No mention of God is found in the book. It is the only Old Testament writing of which not even a fragment was found among the Dead Sea Scrolls. Its original purpose was to exhibit Esther as a model in the service of her nation and to encourage the observance of the Feast of Purim. Deeply embedded in the book is male dominance, even though a woman is featured as its heroine. Queen Vashti is rejected for refusing to obey her husband when he called for her to show her beauty to his drunken guests (1:10-22). Esther replaced Vashti when as a maiden "beautiful

and lovely" (2:7) "the turn came" for her "to go in to
the king" (2:15). It was a man's world; yet here, as at
other times, a woman significantly served or saved
her people.

Nothing directly bears upon the question of age,
but something may be implied by Esther's complete
trust and reliance upon Mordecai, who had "adopted
her as his own daughter" when her father and
mother died (2:5-7). We naturally assume considerable age difference between Mordecai and Esther,
but this is not explicit. In fact, he was not her uncle
but her cousin. Esther was "the daughter of his
uncle" (2:7). Mordecai may have been as old as his
uncle (not uncommon), but nothing to this effect is
said. Age in this book is a "nonissue." That itself
may be significant. Mordecai and Esther are alike in
quality of life, whatever their respective ages.

Job

The book of Job does address the subject of age
directly and significantly. Although isolated passages may leave us with a measure of ambiguity, the
book is strongly affirmative toward long life. Elihu's
speech itself provides a rich study in youth/age relationships, interestingly reserved to the last quarter
of the book (chap. 32—37). God has the last word in
the book (chap. 38—41; 42:7-8); but except for Job,
the young Elihu is the last man to be heard. He
seems to prevail over age; but in the final analysis,
the young man Elihu must come under the same
judgment of God as do his elder counselors Eliphaz,
Bildad, and Zophar (42:7).

The book's most direct tribute to age is in Job's
confession: "Wisdom is with the aged, and understanding in length of days" (12:12). This no doubt

sees age as properly on the side of wisdom. The same perspective appears in Elihu's speech, "Let days speak, and many years teach wisdom" (32:6f). Experience cannot be inherited or borrowed. Other things being equal, age should have the advantage in wisdom and understanding. But other things are not always equal, as can be learned from the book of Job itself. What this book does not support is the idea that age as such is a factor against wisdom and understanding. To be old does not of itself imply that one is "old fogey" or "fuddy-duddy." There is no denigration of age in Job. There is esteem for age.

Just as the book of Job looks for wisdom and understanding in "the aged," it also recognizes that these qualities may fail even there. In a contest with other people, like his three counselors, Job can defend himself: "But I have understanding as well as you; I am not inferior to you" (12:2). The point is that none among us has a monopoly on wisdom and understanding. Job refuses to be intimidated or silenced by anyone, however endowed. Here Job and Elihu (32:6f.) stand together; others are to have their say, but Job and Elihu will have theirs, too. Job's answer probably is with tongue-in-cheek when he replies to Zophar: "No doubt you are the people, and wisdom will die with you" (12:1). Job does not in fact concede final wisdom to anyone except God, and he even contends with God. His basic stance is seen in his confession: "With God are wisdom and might; he has counsel and understanding" (12:13). Such is God's wisdom and might that "He leads counselors away stripped, and judges he makes fools" (12:17) and he "takes away the discernment of the elders" (v. 20). Job's melancholy is that he both affirms God's final wisdom and goodness yet does not understand it. In his agony he dares to contend with God, and he is vindicated for a faith sufficiently honest to contend with God when he does not understand (42:3). Neither the young Elihu nor his elders Eliphaz, Bildad, and Zophar had a corner on wisdom, understanding, or goodness. These qualities belong ultimately to God alone; old age should be on the side of such qualities.

In Job is a basic respect for age. There is no such implication as in modern advertising, that age is ugly and bad and that only youth is beautiful and good. Eliphaz intends to affirm age when he says to Job, "Both the grayhaired and the aged are among us, older than your father" (15:10). They are seen as a proper source of wisdom and understanding. When Job looked back on his "autumn days" (29:4), he probably had in mind his "good life" before being struck by his calamities; but at least the "autumn days" are perceived as ones of beauty and power. They were not empty but full. How old Job was in those "autumn days" is not explicit, but he was old enough to have a harvest of "seven sons and three daughters" (1:2). In any event, Job does not cry out for a return to his youth but remembers his "autumn days." He is not like Ponce de Leon, seeking the fountain of youth; he is a senior adult wanting his family back (29:5). He yearns for those happier days, as he remembers them, "When I went out to the gate of the city, when I prepared my seat in the square, the young men saw me and withdrew, and the aged rose and stood" (29:7-8). Young men deferred to age, and the aged respected their peers. Job's present misery is not alone in his poverty and boils, but in the loss of others' respect: "But now they make sport of me, men who are younger than

I" (30:1). For age to be despised by youth is a crushing blow. Job knows that it is because of his condition and not his age that he is despised, but an added sting is given when despised by men younger than he.

Elihu's speech is highly significant for our study (chap. 32—37). It provides ground for esteeming age, and it also may be a caution against equating quality with quantity of life. It should teach us to listen to age and expect wisdom and goodness from age. It should warn us that qualities good and bad are found in youth and in age. In the final anaiysis, stereotype is to be shunned. The one-factor analysis is to be avoided. The young are not all alike. The aged are not all alike. It is the direction of a life that matters most. Given a right direction, age is a positive factor for good. Given a wrong direction, age is a factor for bad. As seen earlier, it doesn't help when going the wrong way to speed up or even just to keep going. Turn around!

The book takes the position that youth should hear age before it speaks, Elihu waiting until Job and his "three friends" had spoken before he did: "Now Elihu had waited to speak to Job because they were older than he" (32:4). It is proper for youth to hear their elders, and it is proper for the present to hear the past. Other things being equal (and they are not always equal), it is a proper disposition in youth to hear their elders before taking their own stance. The book is equally clear and emphatic in its recognition that the elders are not always worth hearing. Elihu was "angry at Job" because he "justified himself rather than God" (v. 2), and he was "angry at Job's three friends because they had found no answer, although they had declared Job to be in the

wrong" (v. 3). Deference to age did not imply agree-
ment or silence. Elihu challenged Job and the three
older counselors—after hearing them.

Elihu not only gave age the first chance to speak;
he expected wisdom from his elders: "I am young in
years, and you are aged; therefore I was timid and
afraid to declare my opinion to you. I said, 'Let days
speak, and many years teach wisdom'" (vv. 6-7).
That youth *chooses* to let age speak first is commendable of youth. That youth is "timid and afraid"
to declare its opinion in the presence of age is *not* to
the credit of age. The idea that "children are to be
seen and not heard" is itself an idea not deserving a
hearing, except to hear it and reject it. Across a generation gap is fear, but no such gap can stand in the
presence of love, trust, respect, acceptance, and
commitment. If there is a generation gap instead of a
bridge, the heaviest judgment must fall upon age,
although youth has the awesome power of digging
chasms as well as building bridges.

Elihu had a proper instinct when he turned to
"many years" for wisdom (v. 7). Youth has the right
to expect wisdom of older people. That Elihu was
disappointed is explicit. He was disappointed and
angered by what he heard from Job and his three
friends. Elihu correctly saw that wisdom does not
inhere in age as such but in "the spirit in a man" (v.
8*a*). It is in one's openness to God which opens the
way to wisdom: "It is the spirit in a man, the breath
of the Almighty that makes him understand" (v. 8).
Elihu correctly sees, "It is not the old that are wise,
nor the aged that understand what is right" (v. 9).
He does not mean that wisdom and understanding
are not found among the aged but that age itself is
not enough to assure it. Wisdom does not come

through the years themselves but through what one does with the years and what the years do with a person.

Elihu not only correctly rejected the idea that the old are necessarily wise and understanding, he demonstrated that the same holds for youth. Elihu had the right to speak, a basic human right. He also had the compulsion to speak, a normal human need. He is to be supported in his cry, "I must speak, that I may find relief; I must open my lips and answer" (32:20). He properly conceded his limitations: "I too was formed from a piece of clay" (33:6b). Unfortunately, he did not speak as one knowing his fallibility. His pride is bared in the boast, "Bear with me a little, and I will show you, for I have yet something to say on God's behalf" (36:2). It is one thing to confess God's greatness and goodness, but Elihu went further in presuming to be God's guardian. He claimed too much for himself in saying, "For truly my words are not false; one who is perfect in knowledge is with you" (36:4). He hardly escapes the charge he made against those "who are wise in their own conceit" (37:24). Though young, Elihu had the right to speak as well as the need to speak. In speaking he revealed his own limitations, his commonality with old and young alike.

Elihu did not understand Job or the agony of Job. His answers, of which he is so confident and proud, are simplistic, even though they do contain much that is true. They are not answers which have come out of his own struggles with life. They are dogmatic, stock answers which he has inherited. Elihu mouths the very theology which the Book of Job is concerned to refute, that outward circumstances are a sure clue to one's character and piety. Elihu has

lived so little that he believes the fallacy that the evil
die young and the good live long (36:6,14). He believes that "the godless ... die in youth" (vv. 13-14).
He believes that the righteous "complete their days
in prosperity, and their years in pleasantness" (v.
11). By this theology, those who die young automatically are classified as evil, and those who live
long and prosper are classified as good. Had he never
seen babies die? Had he never seen beautiful young
people die? Had he never seen wicked people live far
beyond threescore years and ten, some not even
requiring whatever then substituted for Rolaids? Of
course, he had not seen Jesus on the cross at barely
past thirty! Someone handed Elihu a bag of bad theology (mixed with some that was good), and he didn't
have wisdom or understanding enough to know that
he did not have to carry it like a porter and peddle it
like a salesman. There are old people as lacking in
wisdom and understanding as Elihu, but here youth
was not an advantage.

Elihu's chief limitation came at a point where only
years of agony can help. He condemned Job for con-
tending with God: "Why do you contend against
him, saying, 'He will answer none of my words?' "
(33:13). He glibly branded Job's anguish as "an
empty cry" (35:13) and "empty talk ... words without knowledge" (33:16). Had Elihu never heard of
Moses and Jeremiah in their anguish before God,
crying out their hurts and frustrations as life made
demands upon them beyond their coping power or
wisdom? Of course, he had not heard of Jesus of
Nazareth and his agony from the wilderness to
Gethsemane and the cross. Job was confused but not
wicked (see also 42:7-9). He did contend with God,
but it was out of faith; he trusted God enough to

pour out even his bitterness to God. Job could have identified with the distraught father who cried out to Jesus, "Lord I believe, help thou my unbelief!" (Mark 9:24). Contrary to Elihu, people of faith and piety do often ask in times of trouble, "Where is God my Maker?" (35:10). Almost anyone who has lived long and lived responsibly has asked, "Why?" Elihu condemned Job, but God affirmed Job over against his "three friends": "My wrath is kindled against you [Eliphaz] and against your two friends; for you have not spoken of me what is right, as my servant Job has" (42:7). Surely, it was a chastened Job who was thus vindicated; but Job in his darkest hours was closer to faith and reality than his "three friends" and the young Elihu in all their theologizing and moralizing. Old and young failed to understand Job and the issues of life with which Job struggled. In such struggles, length of years should be to advantage.

The Psalms

The notes most often struck in the Psalms bearing on age are those about the brevity of life, its fragile and transitory nature, and the longing for long life. Little is said or implied as to the effect of age on quality of life. There is no hint of a cult of youth, and long life is seen as a plus.

It is from Psalm 90:10, and there alone in the Bible, that the normal life span is fixed at 70 years, with any extension to 80 seen as exceptional and a bonus: "For the years of our life are threescore and ten, or even by reason of strength fourscore." Almost forgotten is the word ascribed to God in Genesis 6:3: "Then the Lord said, 'My spirit shall not abide in man for ever, for he is flesh, but his days

shall be a hundred and twenty years." Psalm 90:10
has almost totally eclipsed Genesis 6:3, and it may
only be imagined to what extent the prevalence of
the psalmist has psyched us out of what may have
been longer life for many. It has at least been a factor in retirement.

Less well remembered is the mood of Psalm 90,
where verse 10 concludes: "yet their span is but toil
and trouble; they are soon gone, and we fly away."
The whole of Psalm 90 is built around the theme of
God's eternality contrasted with man's transitoriness. Whereas God is God "from everlasting to everlasting" (v. 2), man is turned "back to dust" (v. 3). A
thousand years are to God as yesterday or a watch in
the night, but seventy years, at most eighty, are all
persons have. Persons pass away like a dream or like
the grass (v. 5). "Our years come to an end like a
sigh" (v. 9).

Psalm 90 ends on a happier note for mankind than
it begins. God's eternality and man's transitoriness
should lead to the prayer: "So teach us to number
our days that we may get a heart of wisdom" (v. 12).
Neither brevity nor length of days assures of wisdom, but a realistic acceptance of our limits may occasion the pause that reassesses, becoming a first
step toward wisdom. The psalmist's closing prayer is
for gladness and joy in our days and for meaning,
lasting meaning, to our work (vv. 13-17). The psalm
as a whole, then, is sobered by the acknowledged
brevity of life; but it stands up to it bravely, looking
to God to give it meaning.

Psalm 90 is not isolated in its struggle with the
brevity of life, this being a refrain in the psalms.
Psalm 49 warns that all die, the wealthy as well as
the poor (vv. 6-9), the wise as well as fools (v. 10), the

pompous with all their wealth (vv. 11-12), and those who with "foolish confidence" think they can evade it (vv. 13-14). The psalmist seems to see victory beyond death in saying, "But God will ransom my soul from the power of Sheol, for he will receive me" (v. 15). He closes on another note, warning the rich and pompous that they surely will go down into death, taking nothing with them. Possibly he has only such men in mind in his closing line: "Man cannot abide in his pomp, he is like the beasts that perish" (v. 20). Remembering verse 15, he may mean only that "we can't take it with us."

Psalm 62 is further warning as to the transitory nature of all human life: "Men of low estate are but a breath, men of high estate are a delusion" (9a). When weighed, they weigh out light: "In the balances they go up; they are together lighter than a breath" (9b). The same note is sounded in Psalm 144:4, "Man is like a breath, his days are like a passing shadow." Again, "As for man, his days are like grass; he flourishes like a flower of the field; for the wind passes over it, and it is gone, and its place knows it no more" (Ps. 103:14-16).

Although life is perceived as brief, length of days is desired. There is nothing new in the cry, "Long live the king!" In Psalm 21 "the king" is seen longing for life forever: "He asked life of thee; thou gavest it to him, length of days for ever and ever" (v. 4). It is in a call to a godly life in the fear of God that Psalm 34:12 asks, "What man is there who desires life, and covets many days, that he may enjoy good?" In 61:4 the psalmist prays, "Let me dwell in thy tent for ever! Oh to be safe under the shelter of thy wings!" For "the king" he prays, "Prolong the life of the king: may his years endure to all generations! May he be enthroned for ever before God; bid steadfast love and faithfulness watch over him!" Whether an ordinary king or a messianic king is envisioned and however poetic, at least there is here a reaching out for life without an end. For the one who takes shelter in God is the assurance: "With long life I will satisfy him, and show him my salvation" (Ps. 91:16).

Life is not only seen as brief; there is a fear of aging. Probably the fear of impairment or incapacity is greater than the fear of death itself. There is the fear of helplessness: "Do not cast me off in the time of old age; forsake me not when my strength is spent" (Ps. 71:9). Again, "So even to old age and gray hairs, O God, do not forsake me, till I proclaim thy might to all the generations to come" (v. 18). Awareness of the threat of death is not for the aged alone; it is something with which even the young must cope: "Afflicted and close to death from my youth up, I suffer thy terrors; I am helpless" (88:15). Death is just a heartbeat away from young and old. All are vulnerable to death. The fear of death is less likely to be a problem to one in old age if it is wholesomely faced from youth on. One need not be "morbid" about it. One from earliest days may simply reckon realistically with the fact that death comes sooner or later.

A touch of stereotype may be reflected in Psalm 25:7, "Remember not the sins of my youth, or my transgressions." There is no certain evidence here that the psalmist thinks about "sowing one's wild oats" in youth. With no supporting evidence, it is precarious to read too much into this verse. Youth and age alike are susceptible to sin, but possibly there is here a stereotype as to "the sins of youth." If so, it is corrected in Psalm 119:100, "I understand more than the aged, for I keep thy precepts." Here probably is a recognition that understanding should go with age, but actually it belongs to how one observes God's precepts. Age should be on the side of understanding, but there is no one-to-one relationship between length of years and understanding. The psalmist here clearly shows that the quality of life rests upon deeper foundations than chronology itself. Elders should be wise, but even elders may need to be taught wisdom (Ps. 105:22). That some special responsibility or distinction should characterize "the elders" seems assumed in Psalm 107:32. A more solid note is struck in Psalm 148:12, where praising God should come from "young men and maidens together, old men and children." Silence here as to senior women is probably not a deliberate exclusion.

Proverbs

Wisdom is the unifying theme of this book, and it is tied closer to goodness and responsible choice than to age. The fact that throughout it is a father who lectures to his son implies that wisdom is expected from that side, but this is not an open and shut case. Wisdom and folly may be found at any age or with either sex in the perspectives of Proverbs. For all this, the book is written from the perspective of the adult male. Even so, no single perspective prevails, for balancing lines appear over against any position taken. Stated otherwise, in the book are strong, dogmatic lines; there occur other lines which modify or balance these dogmas. Least balanced is the recurrent scorn poured upon "contentious wives," with no equal time given to scorn for contentious husbands (see also 11:22; 12:4; 18:22; 19:13f.; 21:9,19; 22:14; 25:24; 27:15f.; 30:21-23). The book does close with eulogy for the "good wife," who slaves from dawn until dusk to give her household the best (31:10-31).

In Proverbs wisdom is not automatic with age; it belongs to goodness found in the fear of God: "The fear of the Lord is the beginning of knowledge; fools despise wisdom and instruction" (1:7). Again, "The fear of the Lord is the beginning of wisdom, and the knowledge of the Holy One is insight" (9:10). Throughout the book is the unwavering linkage of goodness and wisdom, evil and folly (see also 8:20; 14:16). Wisdom must be learned or gained. It is not assured by the passing years. It begins with responsible choice and commitment. The book sees age as that which should serve wisdom, but such does not naturally, automatically, or invariably follow.

Proverbs is fully aware of the threat of the generation gap, but its concentration is upon the call to responsible exercise of the parental role (father and mother), with praise for responsible children and scorn for irresponsible children. These themes run throughout the book. Although a male voice speaks throughout the book (see also 4:1; 13:1; 15:5; and other scattered references), both parents are seen as responsible for the upbringing of the children and management of the household: "Hear, my son, your father's instruction; and reject not your mother's teaching" (1:8). What is totally lacking is any explicit addressing of daughters. Instruction in the Law was chiefly for sons, daughters normally being instructed only within the limits of family obligations. Proverbs overcomes male bias at least to the point of recognizing that mothers are to share in the instruction of their sons: "My son, keep your father's commandment, and forsake not your mother's teaching" (6:20; see also 31:1).

Special attention to respect for age appears in 23:22, "Hearken to your father who begot you, and do not despise your mother when she is old." Respect for father and mother is a recurrent demand: "A wise son makes a glad father, but a foolish son is a sorrow to his mother" (see also 15:20; 23:24f.; 28:24; 29:3; 30:11,17). Proverbs gives full recognition to the possibility of children's delinquency (never subscribing to the dogma that there are no delinquent children, only delinquent parents), but its heaviest charge is to the parents. Discipline is seen as parental responsibility, and to shirk it is to invite trouble for the child (13:24; 19:18; 23:13f.; 29:15,17). Equating discipline with not sparing "the rod" is problematic to modern perspective and 23:13 readily raises the specter of child abuse so prevalent today: "Do not withhold discipline from a child; if you beat him with a rod, he will not die." Some children today are literally beaten to death by mothers and fathers, and many are battered in body and spirit by discipline reduced to physical force. Hebrew parents were not characterized by child abuse, and it is important not to equate modern parental brutality with the Hebrew discipline assumed in Proverbs. Motive and manner in discipline is better expressed in 13:24: "He who spares the rod hates his son, but he who loves him is diligent to discipline him." At least love and not hate is to govern discipline, though its ideal is persuasion and not coercion. Violence is improper from either side: "He who does violence to his father and chases away his mother is a son who causes shame and brings reproach" (19:26).

Encouragement is found in the ideal, "Train up a child in the way he should go, and when he is old he will not depart from it" (22:6). Of course, Proverbs knows children who reject the best of parental guidance, just as we do. The faith here is that parental guidance is not wasted, and there is the recognition that the best provision for the quality of old age is in what happens in childhood. It is too late to wait until old age to prepare for it.

Proverbs has a few direct tributes to age: "A hoary head is a crown of glory; it is gained in a righteous life." This is not in the perspective of a cult of youth which finds beauty only in youth. Neither does this see the glory of age as simply a matter of length of years. The glory is in the righteousness which is attained through the years. Again, "The glory of young men is their strength, but the beauty of old men is their gray hair" (20:29). Old people do not have to compete with youth, and gray hair is seen as proper as it is normal to age. The beauty of this verse is that it does not make youth and age competitive: it recognizes the uniqueness and worth of each.

A striking line in its perspective and poetic imagery calls for the highest devotion and fidelity to the aging wife: "Let your fountain be blessed, and rejoice in the wife of your youth, a lovely hind, a graceful doe. Let her affection fill you at all times with delight, be infatuated always with her love" (5:18f.). The writer proceeds to scorn the betrayal of such a wife for the infatuations of some other (vv. 20-23). The view here is that love need not die with age. This is in sharp contrast with such near-contemporary writers to Proverbs as the Romans Plautus and Terence, who limited love to the young and saw it as dead between husband and wife in their old age.[1] There is nothing new about the cult of youth, found clearly in ancient writers, but not here in Proverbs. Marriage between the aged can yet be a relationship of "affection" and "delight."

Ecclesiastes

This is a difficult book, for it appears to be extremely pessimistic or even cynical throughout. To the "Preacher" or "Teacher" *(koheleth)*, "all is vanity and a striving after wind" (1:1,14, and other scattered references). Human existence seems to be determined, and the righteous and unrighteous alike end up in the darkness of Sheol. He even equates the fate of men and beasts, with no advantage to man (3:19f.). The best one can salvage is some enjoyment of what life one has. A more positive note appears in the concluding verses (12:9-14): "Fear God, and keep his commandments; for this is the whole duty of man. For God will bring every deed into judgment, with every secret thing, whether good or evil" (vv. 13-14). These lines must certainly be given utmost prominence as to the book's intention.

Overshadowing the whole book is the preoccupation with the brevity of life and its inevitable end in Sheol (5:18). Man lives in uncertainty "the few days of his vain life, which he passes like a shadow" (6:12). Even long life offers the Teacher little promise: "Even though he should live a thousand years twice told [2,000 years], yet enjoy no good — do not all go to the one place?" (6:6). He can even say that better is "the day of death, than the day of birth" (7:1). The Teacher warns that even in long life one needs to remember its end: "For if a man lives many years, let him rejoice in them all; but let him remember that the days of darkness will be many. All that comes is vanity" (11:8). The "days of darkness" may mean Sheol or senility (see also 12:1-8).

The saddest lines in the book are in the closing section in which he pictures the decline which he sees as preceding death in old age (12:1-8). This is a picture of life extended beyond meaning, when in one's declining years one says, "I have no pleasure in them" (v. 1). In highly poetic and symbolic language, the Teacher seems to describe failing eyesight, weakened limbs, loss of teeth, interrupted sleep, fear and insecurity, loss of natural bodily drives, etc. This he sees as the pitiful stage leading to death. Old age can be like that, and often it is.

Most of the questions raised in this book must find answer elsewhere; as, indeed, such answers may be found in other biblical books. Probably the nearest approach in the book to some guidance as to the matter of age and aging is found in chapters 11—12. In 11:9 the Teacher encourages the "young man" to rejoice in his youth, evidently to him the best part of life, but at that time to recognize the fact that God will hold one accountable for what he does in or with his youth. The Teacher does not make the point, but it does follow that the best provision one can make for old age is in what one does with one's youth. This may not be the Teacher's point, for he seems even here to take the pessimistic view: "for youth and the dawn of life are vanity" (v. 10).

Chapter 12 begins on what promises to be a thoroughly constructive note: "Remember also your Creator in the days of your youth" (v. 1a). On this foundation it could be urged that youth is the best time to prepare for age and that it is under God that this must be done. What follows is not this line of reasoning but rather a dismal picture of the decline of life into a helpless and meaningless state. Of course, many in old age suffer such fate, whether because of their own negligence or due to biological causes over which they can do nothing and about which medical science can do little or nothing. Senility is not a proper subject for joking. It is as sad as the condition described by the Teacher. It is not inevitable. Many live into a ripe old age with the terminal years richer and more joyful than even the early years. Barring such as arteriosclerosis, about which sometimes little can be done, one does have options in determining the quality of old age. Youth is the time to begin working at this. Whatever the Teacher may have intended in his admonition to youth, he is profoundly right in the urgency of his injunction: "Remember also your Creator in the days of your youth." To forget in youth is to take a giant step toward the pitiful state described by the Teacher.

The Song of Solomon

This is a love song, a man and a woman singing their love for and to one another. So uninhibited is the expression of the craving of each for the other, leaving little to the imagination, that attempts have been made to allegorize the book or in some other way overcome its unabashed enjoyment of sexuality. It is the enjoyment of the normal and wholesome love of a man and a woman for one another, with special attention to love in its sensual expression. The human body is seen as beautiful, and the deep drive of each for the other is recognized without shame or apology. There is not a hint of promiscuity, for each seeks the other and none other. Although marriage is not explicit, there is no hint that it is to be flaunted. That the book has its focus on the bodily expression of human love does not imply that there are no other dimensions to love or to human fulfillment. No book need be encyclopedic or definitive; and here is a biblical book which gives full attention to a primary aspect of personhood much exploited, often neglected, and sometimes considered tabu in circles of piety.

Along with the unusual candor of the book on a sensitive subject is its almost unparalleled recognition in Jewish literature of woman's sexuality. The book simply assumes that the sexual drive is as deep in woman as in man, and it assumes it to be normal and right for each to seek fulfillment in the other. In a passage of rare candor, Paul recognized the sexual rights of a wife as equal to those of a husband (1 Cor. 7:3-5). Paul is explicit in affirming that "conjugal rights" belong to wife and husband equally, and it is a fraud for either to deny such to the other. The Song of Solomon is devoted in its entirety to this aspect of the man/woman relationship, not as a defense of the right but as a celebration of the privilege. It is in no sense chauvinistic. It gives equal attention to the woman and the man, with neither dominant over the other. Nowhere is "sexism" more completely overcome than in this celebration of the drive of the sexes toward one another (see also Gen. 2:24).

What about "agism" in the Song of Solomon? Since the lovers in this poem are pictured as young, the book could be understood as restricting love to the young. Since the lovers are also strikingly beautiful, the book could be understood as restricting love to the beautiful. Probably neither is intended.

There is no overt or seemingly intentional agism in the poem. There is nothing as to a generation gap. In fact there is nothing about older people at all. In this is the possible problem. There are in the book the ingredients for "agism." The book can be so understood as to serve "the cult of youth." Throughout, the lovers are young and beautiful. If the implication is that love is normal only to the young and the beautiful, then a lot of people are left out, young and old. There are alternate ways of understanding the book. That these particular lovers are young and beautiful does not necessarily imply that lovers may not be old and/or uncomely. It is our contention that love, including its sensual expression, belongs to the old as well as the young and also to the uncomely, whether young or old.

An old proverb has it that "Beauty is in the eye of the beholder." The Song of Solomon may be understood as building upon this romantic principle, by which each lover is beautiful to the other. Love has the art of removing the blemishes from the beloved, either by accepting and including them in the affirmation of the beloved or by transforming them. Taken this way, the Song of Solomon makes room for all of us, whatever our ages or wherever we place on the scale of one to ten as the movie business rates beauty. In this perspective, to every lover the beloved is a Number 10.

But we must reckon seriously with the perspective that love is, indeed, for the young and beautiful, normally if not exclusively. That was an ancient perspective. For example, the Roman dramatist Terence (185-159 BC) saw love as exclusively between young men and women. In his plays marriage for people in their senior years is always loveless, drab, and ugly. To Terence, youth is beautiful and age is ugly. Modern advertising employs this stereotype. Almost always it has youth and beauty associated with the good and age associated with the bad. The Song of Solomon probably does not intend this stereotype, but it could be taken that way.

The Song of Solomon does glamorize its lovers, however interpreted. Have you read it recently? The woman is in the full development of her body, not a girl before she has blossomed: "We have a little sister, and she has no breasts. What shall we do for our sister, on the day when she is spoken for?" (8:8). The obvious implication is that the little sister has a problem now, and if she does not develop she will have a real problem. The song is about one whose "two breasts" are like "two fawns, twins of a gazelle" (7:3) or like "clusters" from a palm tree (7:7). The male lover, too, is young and handsome. His lover thus sees him, "As an apple tree among the trees of wood, so is my beloved among young men" (2:3). Again, "My beloved is like a gazelle, or a young stag" (2:9). No place is made for anything but youth and beauty: "Until the day breathes and the shadows flee, turn, my beloved, be like a gazelle, or a young stag upon rugged mountains" (2:17). The young lover may be ruddy, black-haired, or curly-headed, but he is not bald-headed: "My beloved is all radiant and ruddy, distinguished among ten thousand. His head is the finest gold; his locks are wavy, black as a raven" (5:10-11). The very last line in the book places the accent upon youth: "Make haste, my beloved, and be like a gazelle or a young stag upon the mountains of spices" (8:14).

There can be no quarrel with the celebration of the love between a woman and a man in the prime of their sexuality. There can be no doubt as to biological processes which bring male and female to full potency and then diminish. There can be no quarrel with idealizing the beloved, with every beloved one in perfect beauty in the eyes of the lover. What generally is more assumed than valid is the idea that sexuality or love in its sexual expression is primarily if not exclusively for the young. The Song of Solomon does not fall into the stereotype as found in Terence, wherein the old are always drab, ugly, and loveless. It does not denigrate the old; but for whatever reason, it remains silent with respect to older people. It is our responsibility not to fall into the stereotype that love is for the physically young and beautiful alone or even primarily. Not all young people are glamour girls or glamour boys; but they have their rights and needs, and they have their capacity for love. The needs and capacities of older people are real and as important to them as for any age group. Let not the image makers in television, cinema, or advertising get away with the stereotype that makes love the exclusive right of the flower of only one age group.

Worse even than the idea that love and sexuality are for the beautiful and the young alone is the stereotype which sees sexuality as abnormal, inappropriate, or even vulgar in the older years. Frequently heard is the expression "a dirty old man." With the same behavior, a young man is not called "a dirty young man." If the expression "a dirty old woman" has not emerged it probably is because the stereotypers and phrase-makers have just omitted "old women," simply assuming that they are not interested. What we are saying is that every human being has the right to be, and such right is both privilege and responsibility. Sexuality, with its fulfillment and its dangers, belongs to women and men alike, as the Song of Solomon has it. It belongs to young and old, the glamorous and the unglamorous, a matter beyond the concerns of the Song of Solomon but a proper extension of its concerns.

4
Age in the Prophets

The books examined in this chapter belong largely to the middle section of the Hebrew canon, consisting of the latter prophets, both the Major and Minor (Twelve) Prophets. Following the English order, Daniel is included in this chapter although it appears in "the Writings" in the Hebrew canon. The question of the unity of various prophetic books is under continuing debate, but the books will be examined in turn in the form in which they now appear. What is concluded in critical research on structural problems affects one's understanding of the sequence in which certain perspectives on age may have occurred, but the perspectives themselves are embedded in the books as they stand. To some extent, the perspective of a book itself as it stands can be isolated.

Isaiah

The 66 chapters of this book seem to fall into three major sections (1—39; 40—55; 56—66), although scholarly opinion differs as to the structure of the book. Probably chapters 1—39 are to be understood against the background of the Assyrian threat to Israel in the eighth century BC, chapters 40—55 against the background of the Babylonian exile in the sixth century BC, and chapters 56—66 against

the background of the early postexilic period.[1]
Change in historical setting, at least from Assyrian
to Babylonian threat, is explicit. There seem also to
be variant perspectives along with much commonality running through the book as it stands. Whether
the perspectives of a single lifespan or those of several centuries, they significantly bear on the subject
of age. Nowhere is age discussed as a subject in its
own right, but significant perspectives appear both
in explicit and implicit form.

It may be significant that in each of the three
major sections there is explicit concern for the disadvantaged (see also 29:18-19; 35:3-7; 42:7,18-22;
49:9-10; 58:6-7; 61:1-9), but the aged are not explicitly named in such lists. The aged may be implied in
reference to "the weak hands" and "the feeble
knees" (35:3), but this is questionable. That there is
here a special reference to the aged is unlikely, for
elsewhere such phrases apply to all ages: "Therefore
all hands will be feeble, and every man's heart will
melt" (13:7). Terror, not age, is implied in this latter
passage, all humans fearing when "the day of the
Lord comes" (13:9).

Various other conditions of privation or disadvantage are explicit in descriptions of God's merciful
redemption. In 29:18-19 special feeling is shown
toward the deaf, the blind, the meek, and the poor.
In 35:3-7 "the weak hands" are to be strengthened
and "the feeble knees" are to be made firm. In 42:7
the eyes of the blind are to be opened and the prisoners set free from dungeons and darkness. In
42:18-22 the concern is for the deaf, the blind, those
robbed and plundered, and those "trapped in holes
and hidden in prisons." In 49:9-10 God's pity is extended to prisoners and those who hunger and thirst.

In 58:6-7 true "fasting" is defined in terms of loosing the bonds of wickedness, undoing the thongs of the yoke, letting the oppressed go free, sharing one's bread with the hungry, bringing the homeless poor into one's house, and clothing the naked. In 61:1-9, where Jesus found a model for his self-interpretation and mission, concern is explicit for the afflicted, the brokenhearted, the captives in prison and in other forms of bondage, those who mourn, and the aliens and foreigners. Such concern follows when "the Spirit of the Lord God" comes upon one, when one has been "anointed" by the Lord (61:1).

In all these beautiful passages of concern, there is no explicit or unambiguous reference to the aged. Silence on the subject may be explained variously. Already recognized is the possibly implicit reference in some of the descriptions; but the fact remains, age is not explicit. It could imply that there was no normal or characteristic neglect of the aged in Israel, even though the Babylonians are indicted for ill-treatment of the aged (47:6). Generally, age was esteemed in Israel. Another possibility is that the sensitivity level was not sufficient to call attention to the aged. Even goodwill sometimes overlooks groups in society needing special attention, not deliberately but because it is difficult to be sensitized and responsive to all valid claims upon us. As with racism, sexism, and other areas of discrimination or neglect, such easily follows as to agism. We cannot say why the aged are not named along with others who are made explicit in the concern of these passages. In any event, there always are those about us who rightfully claim our special attention, and many aged people are among them.

Interestingly, it is in the middle section (chaps.

40—55) that concern for the aged is explicit. The inhumanity of Babylonian rule is seen as falling especially upon the aged: "On the aged you made your yoke exceedingly heavy" (47:6). As prisoners of war in Babylon, the aged especially came in for harsh treatment, and the writer protests such inhumanity. In 40:30-31 it is seen that "Even youths shall faint and be weary, and young men shall fall exhausted"; but the main point is that our real strength comes from the Lord. Those who "wait for the Lord" are those who in the exchange of their weakness for his strength are able to "run and not be weary" and to "walk and not faint." This is a clear recognition that there are dimensions of strength unrelated to age as such. Although physically, the advantage belongs to youth and even the young require strength from above; and this strength belongs not to young or old as such, but to those who wait, not passively but with the eagerness of a farmer awaiting a harvest (Kelley, p. 302), whatever one's age.

A further passage in chapters 40—55 reflects explicit concern for the aged: "Hearken to me, O house of Jacob, all the remnant of the house of Israel, who have been borne by me from birth, carried from the womb; even to your old age I am He, and to gray hairs I will carry you" (46:3-4). The emphasis here is upon the faithfulness of God, whose promised care is from birth to death; but it is noteworthy that the aged are mentioned. In 51:12 human mortality is openly faced, but it is done so constructively. Man is seen as one "who dies" and "the son of man" (poetic parallelism) as "made like grass." This does not intend to be pessimistic or to imply a special problem for the aged. All honest people, at whatever age, live with the realization that death comes sooner or later. The intention of this passage is to reassure, for one who knows God's comfort need not fear death. The writer is sensitive to a human need for assurance, at whatever age. It does appear that if anywhere in Isaiah there is deliberate attention to the aged, it is in the middle section (chaps. 40—55).

There is no negativity toward age as such in chapters 1—39, and there is some attention to it. In 3:2 "the elder" seems to represent a public office or role. The point of the context is the indictment of Judean society for its disintegration. Marks of such decadence include such breakdown as that "the youth will be insolent to the elder" (v. 5). Overall what is described is the breakdown of the structures of society and the collapse of law and order, but one mark of it is disrespect for older people.

In fairness, elders along with princes come in for heavy judgment because of their betrayal of the trust placed in them as leaders of the people: "The Lord enters into judgment with the elders and princes of his people: 'It is you who have devoured the vineyard, the spoil of the poor is in your houses. What do you mean by crushing my people, by grinding the face of the poor?' says the Lord God of hosts." The aged are vulnerable not only to the injustice of being oppressed; they are capable of being the oppressors. It requires no scientific research to observe the obvious role of many older people in human exploitation and oppression. Much power, economic and political, is in physically feeble hands.

In 9:8-17 is a heavy indictment upon all Israel, where failure is such that the Lord will cut off from Israel "head and tail" (v. 14), the "head" being "the

elder and honored man" and the "tail" being "the
prophet who teaches lies." Failure is seen in all these
leaders, elders included. Judgment will fall upon
trusted leaders, and the "young men" as well as the
"fatherless and widows" (v. 17) will suffer from such
failure of the elders. The "elders" should be responsible leaders and "prophets" should speak for God;
but both are vulnerable to failure, and in their failing
all suffer. This is not discrimination against the
elders; it is the application of the principle that from
him to whom much is given much is required. In
14:21 is implied yet another way in which older
people may sin against younger people: "Prepare
slaughter for his sons because of the guilt of their
fathers, lest they rise and possess the earth, and fill
the face of the world with cities." Understood as vengeance, arbitrarily punishing one generation for the
sins of a foregoing one, the overriding correctives of
Jesus Christ must be heard, "But I say unto you"
(Matt. 5:28-43). Understood as the all too familiar pattern of the sins of the parents living on in their children, or the older generation infecting the younger
generation with its inhumanity, the passage is elo-
quent and to the point. Parents can be the boon or
the bane of their children, and the "older generation" can be the making or the undoing of the ones
to follow. This is the realism of 14:21.

"Baldness" in 15:2 and 22:12 probably implies
cultic shaving of the head, along with the wearing of
sackcloth as symbols of mourning or repentance.
This, then, carries no necessary implication of scorn
or disrespect for the aged (baldness in fact can occur
quite early in life). The humiliation here is that of
"young and old" in Babylonian exile, "naked and
barefoot, with buttocks uncovered!" (20:4), with no

age discrimination. The humiliation is in their captivity, the dehumanization being the common plight of young and old. Some special dignity is probably implied for "the elders" when the Lord reasserts his reign in Mount Zion "and before his elders he will manifest his glory" (24:23). That longevity or at least a full life is universally desired, if life is desired at all, is supported by 38:5,10, where King Hezekiah longs for the extension of life and that he not have to depart into Sheol in "the noontide" of his days. Of course, there are factors which can modify this longing: a sense of meaninglessness under impairment or a sense of meaninglessness in terms of self-image or purpose.

On the positive side, faith in meaningful life beyond death frees one from the overriding factor in Hezekiah's shrinking back from death, his understanding of death as being "consigned to the gates of Sheol for the rest of my years." Isaiah struggles with the question of death; and though there is not the full victory over death as appears in the New Testament, he did anticipate it to this extent: "He will swallow up death for ever, and the Lord God will wipe away tears from all faces, and the reproach of his people he will take away all the earth; for the Lord has spoken" (25:8). Even stronger is his assurance, "Thy dead shall live, their bodies shall rise. O dwellers in the dust, awake and sing for joy! For thy dew is a dew of light, and on the land of the shades thou wilt let it fall" (26:19). Where this faith prevails, death loses its terror for young and old. Hezekiah's faith seems to have given him no such victory.

Section 3 (chaps. 56—66) contains little bearing upon age. In 62:5 marriage and its joys could be perceived as coextensive with youth, reflecting a youth cult mentality, but this is not the likely intention. The passage is poetic and must not be pressed logically, else the "sons" of Zion are married to their mother! Obviously, the poetry does not intend such pedantries of logic. Neither is there any necessary bias toward youth. The emphasis is upon the "virginity" of the "bride," not upon the age of the bridegroom. What is required in God's people is purity, not a certain age bracket.

Deliberate perspective on longevity is explicit in 65:20, where in the "new heavens and a new earth" (65:17) it is seen: "No more shall there be in it an infant that lives but a few days, or an old man who does not fill out his days, for the child shall die a hundred years old, and the sinner a hundred years old shall be accursed" (v. 20). This is not the Heaven of Christian faith; it is life on earth where there yet is birth and death, good and evil. What is envisioned is a newly created world here on earth. Emphasis is placed upon the expectation of long life for the righteous. Kelley so interprets it: "One who attains a mere hundred years will still be considered a child, while one who fails to attain a hundred years will be regarded as one under a curse" (p. 370). That length of life corresponds to one's moral quality is not supported by the fact of infant mortality on the one hand and on the other longevity in many who are wicked. To turn this around, judging the quality of life by its length, faces such untenable conclusions as that Joseph Stalin (who lived long) was more righteous than the millions of young people whom he sent to early death, or that Adolf Hitler (who lived 56 years) was more righteous than Anne Frank (who died as a child). To reduce this vision to prose is a disaster; to recognize in it human longing for long and

meaningful life is to hear a significant word out of
the distant past which yet captures the longing of us
all.

Jeremiah

Jeremiah's prophetic ministry spanned the reigns
of three kings in Judah: Josiah (627-609 BC), Jeoiakim
(609-598 BC), and Zedekiah (597-587 BC), plus the
governorship of Gedaliah (587 BC) and beyond. As
was normal for a prophet, his preaching was directed to the power structures of state and religion
as well as to the people. Jeremiah was a fearless
prophet, especially in his realism which placed him
over against prophets and priests who gave blind
allegiance to the king in what now would be called
"civil religion," where religion simply tries to give
sanction to the state. Jeremiah never addressed the
subject of old age or the subject of agism itself. The
book does have some rewarding passages which il-
luminate our study.

Jeremiah's call to the prophetic ministry came
early, probably at the age of 20 or soon after. He
shrank back from the call, making the protest: "Ah,
Lord God! Behold, I do not know how to speak, for I
am only a youth." It is understandable and commendable that a youth of about 20 would be fright-
ened by so awesome a commission as was his: "I
appointed you a prophet to the nations" (v. 5). Jeremiah's call and commission do discount any stereotype which would limit the credentials of awesome
responsibility to any one age group. Openness to
God and to the resources for life and ministry count
more than calendar age. This is not to overlook the
fact that years should work for and not against
maturation and fulfillment. Agism robs older people

of their rights; this passage affirms the rights of youth. Not to be overlooked is the fact that after forty years or more, the battered prophet preached at maximum power.

Throughout the book of Jeremiah is the recognition that the law of sin and its wages works impartially against young and old alike (see also 6:11; 13:14; 51:22). Jeremiah saw guilt and suffering to fall impartially upon young and old, men and women. Unfortunately, innocent victims suffer some of the results with the guilty, as in the exile, where "children in the street" (apparently little children at play) and "the old folk and the very old" are included among those deported (6:11). Sin occurs in youth or age; suffering falls in some way upon guilty and innocent, at whatever age.

Patterns in old age are sometimes traceable from youth. In 22:21 such is explicit: "I spoke to you in prosperity, but you said, 'I will not listen.' This has been your way from your youth, that you have not obeyed my voice." The charge is made against the nation, but the pattern is found in the individual. No lesson from our study is clearer than that the quality of old age is largely determined in youth. That by no means implies that character and life-style cannot be modified or reversed at any stage of life, even into old age; but it does mean that the odds diminish with the passing years. Not only does delay heighten the risk but it robs the earlier years of what at best is discovered or recovered toward the end of life.

Comparison of 19:1ff. with 26:17 is instructive. In 19:1, Jeremiah is told to act out a prophetic parable in the presence of "some of the elders of the people and some of the senior priests." Of these it should be right to expect wisdom, maturity, and integrity of action. As the story unfolds, nothing is said as to their responsible action, and apparently they were negative toward Jeremiah's message. At least, when Pashhur the priest "beat Jeremiah the prophet, and put him in the stocks" (20:1), there is no hint that the elders and senior priests were dissociated from such evil action.

By contrast, "the elders of the land" cited in 26:19 come through positively in a crisis situation. Jeremiah had been condemned by "the priests and the prophets," and they wanted him sentenced to death. Then "the princes" protested that Jeremiah did not deserve to be sentenced to death, to which stand "the elders of the land" gave their support. Jeremiah thus was condemned by the clergy and defended by the laymen. The point of our concern, however, is with the age factor. The elders put the crisis over Jeremiah in historical perspective, reminding their hearers of past occasions when a prophet who spoke an unpleasant truth was not condemned by the head of state. It does not follow that young people cannot or do not know history, but in this story age proved to be on the side of knowledge, perspective, and justice.

From these two stories comes a caution against stereotype. In one story the elders did nothing for justice and may have helped thwart it. In the other story the elders were knowledgeable and just. Age should always be an advantage, but age is not enough. As seen before, it is the direction of a life which determines whether the years work for or against the quality of life.

Chapters 29—31 supply another dimension of life proper to older people even as to young people. It is the continuing pursuit of life within its viable limits and the celebration of life as that which is appropriate. The senior years are not just for survival. For some older people it does become a matter of survival, just holding on; but the same may be true for a child or a young person. Disease or injury may bring impairment at any age, just as one may become worn out by the passing years. In extreme impairment, whether in youth or advanced age, survival may be the only option. That is not a decision made but a situation imposed. However, where options are still there, it is as proper for older persons to go on with life and to celebrate it as it is for young people. Such is the advice to "the elders of the exiles" (29:1).

The exiles, among whom were included "elders," were admonished to resume life to the fullest upon being sent from Jerusalem to Babylon: "Thus says the Lord of hosts, the God of Israel, to all the exiles whom I have sent into exile from Jerusalem to Babylon: Build houses and live in them; plant gardens and eat their produce. Take wives and have sons and daughters in marriage, that they may bear sons and daughters; multiply there, and do not decrease. But seek the welfare of the city where I have sent you into exile, and pray to the Lord on its behalf, for in its welfare you will find your welfare" (29:4-7).

Obviously, "the elders" would not be able to do all of this, but the same would hold for others. The idea is clear enough. Even in exile, life was to go on. So with elders today, retirement need not be a "Babylonian exile." The later years could be more meaningful for many older people were they not psyched out of living on a beyond retirement life as normal as possible. This is not to suggest that meaningful life and activity are one and the same. Older people do not have to earn their right to be here; they do not have to produce in order to achieve their right to be. They have worth as they are. Some want to curtail life and may need to do so. The point from Jeremiah, however, is that life does not have to stop because of a change as abrupt as exile—or retirement.

In chapter 31 is anticipated a happy return from exile, and celebration is prescribed for the event: "Then shall the maidens rejoice in the dance, and the young men and the old shall be merry. I will turn their mourning into joy, I will comfort them, and give them gladness for sorrow" (v. 13). Celebration is for the old and not just for the young. Not only is celebration proper to the senior years, it may well be a factor in extending them. Should one protest that "celebration" (abused) may shorten life, that follows; but the same holds for celebration in youth, if abused. There is a true celebration which is on the side of life, both in its quality and length.

A final lesson may be found in the bemoaning of Ephraim, who cried out to God for restoration: "For after I had turned away I repented; and after I was instructed, I smote upon my thigh; I am ashamed, and I was confounded, because I bore the disgrace of my youth" (31:19). The shame that leads to repentance belongs properly to restoration to the Lord and to meaningful life. To remember "the disgrace" of one's youth as a step toward repentance is proper and salutary. To keep on remembering "the disgrace of my youth" is for anyone of us an injustice to ourselves, at whatever age. Once repented and forgiven, the sins of youth are to be forgotten. It is not a right thing for older people to carry to their graves sins of youth long since confessed. Self-affirmation and a wholesome love of self is proper, once sins of any age have been repented.

Lamentations

This book gets its English title from 2 Chronicles
35:25, where the lament of Jeremiah for Josiah is
taken to refer to this work. The five laments probably are liturgical hymns looking back on the destruction of Jerusalem by the Babylonians in 587 BC
but before the release of the captives in 538 BC.[2]
These are five poetic laments, produced apparently in and for liturgical use. Four of the poems are
formed as an acrostic on the twenty-two letters of
the Hebrew alphabet, and the fifth poem is comprised of twenty-two lines or stanzas, though not
acrostic. Probably the laments were sung liturgi-
cally in services relating to the tragic events of the
Exile. Lamentations is a struggle of faith with the
realities of sin, judgment, defeat, and suffering. The
laments reach out for understanding and hope.
As is true in many biblical books, the subject of
age is not an agenda item in its own right in Lamentations, but some perspectives come through in at
least incidental reference. The overriding lesson
here for the question of age may be the impartiality
of suffering in the wake of departure from trust in
God. Suffering falls upon all, from infants to the
aged: "In the dust of the streets lie the young and
the old" (2:21). If "the elders" of Zion "sit on the
ground in silence," with dust on their heads and
clothed in sackcloth, so do "the maidens of Jerusalem" have their heads bowed to the ground (2:10)
and "infants and babes faint in the streets of the
city" (v. 11). Dehumanization can be such that even
normally "compassionate women" feed upon "their
own children" (4:10), shockingly gruesome whether
literal or figurative; but in such human failure there

likewise is "no favor to the elders" (4:16). When a nation forsakes God, it abandons its own humanity, and all lose, from little babies to the aged.

Lamentations has a special feeling for "the elders," but not at the expense of any other age group. Many of the laments express the hurt of "the elders." In her distress, Jerusalem cries out for help, but in vain, for her "lovers" deceived her and her "priests and elders perished in the city, while they sought food to revive their strength" (1:19). In the defeat and humiliation of Jerusalem, "no respect is shown to the elders" (5:12); and "The old men have quit the city gate" (5:14). The aged have been robbed of their role and their dignity.

A note of sober judgment appears in the charge: "Our fathers sinned, and are no more; and we bear their iniquities" (5:7). Privilege always carries with it responsibility. In their failures, parents and older people hurt both themselves and those who follow them. A redemptive note is sounded in 3:25-27. Each line of this stanza begins with the word "good" in the Hebrew text. Patient waiting upon the Lord is assured of the salvation (v. 26) which God's steadfast love (v. 22) will bring about. However long or difficult the waiting, one who patiently waits upon the Lord "will not be cast off forever" by his steadfast love (vv. 28-33).

In the midst of this long passage (vv. 22-36) is the striking assurance: "It is good for a man that he bear the yoke in his youth" (v. 27). Of course, the earlier one learns to wait patiently upon the Lord, the better. Possibly implied is the basic truth that it generally is in youth that life patterns are set. Whether that is the intention of the verse or not, it does follow that the quality of old age is best assured when in youth one learns to bear God's "yoke," that is, come under God's discipline by becoming his disciple.

Ezekiel

Writing up the appearance of age in the book of Ezekiel is not a happy assignment for a book which intends to inform and sensitize with respect to age and aging, but credibility requires integrity, whether pleasant or not. There is no honest or competent way in which the senior years can be equated with good. Like any other age, senior adults can be good or evil, wise or foolish, authentic or phony. Quality seniority does not just happen; it must be cultivated. "Elders" are cited about eight times in Ezekiel, but only once favorably, and they are "foreigners" cited for their craftsmanship in caulking ships (27:9)!

Throughout Ezekiel "the elders of Judah" and "the elders of Israel" are pictured as unfaithful to God, worshipers of false gods, and without counsel for the people. They go through the motions of inquiring of God, but they hear no word from God. Along with the prophets, priests, and princes, they are the established leaders of the people; but they fail miserably in their role. To follow them is disaster (7:26). They are not false because they are old, but they are demonstration of the fact that age is not enough. Their failure was in what they did with their options, and for their failure they are required to bear the guilt. Ezekiel rejected the theology of determinism which passes the buck of responsibility, rejecting the proverb "The fathers have eaten sour grapes, and the children's teeth are set on edge" (18:2), warning rather that "the soul that sins shall die" (18:4). Ezekiel also warned that for trusted

leaders to be unfaithful to their commission brings
upon them the "blood" of them whom they failed to
guide (3:18 and other scattered references). In such
context, "the elders" in the book of Ezekiel failed
miserably and incurred the heaviest possible guilt.

Ezekiel was another prophet of the Babylonian
exile. In fact, he was a priest and son of a priest, a
prophet, and a "watchman" for the exiles. He lived
through the destruction of Jerusalem (587 BC), and
preached judgment and hope as he shared person-
ally in the exile. He represents probably a stage in
the transition from prophecy to apocalypse, and his
heavy use of symbolism and allegory makes him
sometimes hard to follow. At one point, however, he
is crystal clear: "the elders" are so unfaithful and
apostate that they cut themselves off from any fruit-
ful inquiry of God.

Ezekiel's initial reference to "the elders" is in a
context indicting four classes of leadership: prophets, priests, elders, and kings/princes: "Disaster
comes upon disaster, rumor follows rumor; they seek
a vision from the prophet, but the law perishes from
the priest, and counsel from the elders. The king
mourns, the prince is wrapped in despair, and the
hands of the people of the land are palsied by terror"
(7:26-27). Precisely what Jeremiah's opponents said
could not happen did happen, for vision, knowledge
of the law, and counsel did "perish" in or from
prophet, priest, and elder (Jer. 18:18).

In 8:1 "the elders of Judah" are found sitting with
Ezekiel in his house. The place of the elder thus is
reestablished in the exile, presumably implying that
it was a structure in society in happier times now
thought worth continuing. We are not told what
they were doing there, and subsequent reference

has nothing positive to say about them. In 8:11-12 seventy of "the elders of the house of Israel" (the same as those of Judah?), are seen to be engaged in "vile abominations" (v. 9). These elders were seen as engaged in various acts of pagan worship, worshiping murals of creeping things, the sun, and various pagan gods (vv. 12-18). Some of their worship was done "in the dark" (v. 12), in keeping with the esoteric nature of some of the pagan practice. Such was the apostasy of "the elders." Aging did not help these men! In the judgment which followed, all ages suffered destruction, and it "began with the elders" (9:6).

In 14:1 "certain of the elders of Israel" come to Ezekiel, apparently seeking some word from Yahweh; but instead they receive a message of judgment. The indictment was that "these men have taken their idols into their hearts" (v. 3). Overtly, their "gods" did not exist; but they were self-destroyed in what they took into their hearts as their gods. These were not inexperienced youths; these were "the elders." In 20:1 again "certain of the elders of Israel came to inquire of the Lord." They were seeking some oracle from Yahweh, but Yahweh had no word for them, except a word of judgment through his prophet. It is not that God was unwilling to hear; he was unwilling to be used by these apostate "elders."

Only in 27:9 are "elders" affirmed in Ezekiel, and these are "the elders of Gebal," men skilled in caulking the seams of a ship. Gebal (Byblos) was a Phoenician coastal city, famed among other things for able seamen and master builders. Gebal had a history dating several millennia BC, often destroyed and rebuilt, and a melting pot of many cultures.[3] Precisely who these "elders of Gebal" were is not disclosed. They are identified only by craft, and they appear to be good at it. Old need not imply incompetence.

In summary, the book of Ezekiel does yield valuable insight on age and aging, even though for the most part the elders appear in a bad light. The "elders of Israel" serve as a warning that aging does not of itself produce quality. Through years alone one may either mellow or sour. Older people may turn out like the elders of Israel but they need not. On the happier side, "the elders of Gebal" were still highly functional in their craft. With old age one may lose one's skill, but this varies with the individual. The elders of Gebal are not unique, for there is no fixed calendar age—whether 65 or 70 or whatever—at which one can no longer caulk a ship or exercise the skills of one's vocation.

Daniel

It would be going too far to find in the book of Daniel a "cult of youth," but there is here at least some hint of it. If in Ezekiel the judgment falls most heavily upon "the elders," in Daniel those most esteemed are youths. The heroes of the book are Daniel and his three companions Hananiah, Mishael, and Azariah (1:6). In fact, these four youths belonged to a group of young Hebrews of unspecified number who were taken captive from Jerusalem to Babylon when Nebuchadnezzer captured Jerusalem; and they are described as "youths without blemish, handsome and skillful in all wisdom, endowed with knowledge, understanding, learning, and competent to serve in the king's palace, and to teach them the letters and language of the Chal-

deans" (1:4). That they were "youths" is emphatic
(1:4,10,15,17), although their specific ages are not
given. Their excellence is described in terms of physical appearance, moral integrity and courage, wisdom, and trust in God.

Daniel and his young companions are portrayed
over against "the wise men of Babylon," presumably older men. These established counselors in
Babylon are variously entitled wise men, Chaldeans,
enchanters, sorcerers, and astrologers (2:2,27; 4:7;
5:7,11), the terms apparently used synonymously.[4]
These "wise men of Babylon" are not charged with
moral failure; they simply could not deliver upon
demand. They could not meet the king's call for in-
terpreting his dreams. Daniel, the youth, succeeded
where they failed. Daniel was prompt to disavow
personal credit, ascribing his success to a revelation
from God. Of course, his openness to God was his
part in the happy result. As a consequence, he was
placed over "the wise men of Babylon" (2:48).

This book does not ascribe Daniel's wisdom to his
youth but to his trust in God. The book does not
ascribe the incompetence of "the wise men of Babylon" to their age (it is not specified); by implication,
at least, it was because they did not trust the true
God. Aging should be on the side of wisdom as seen
already; but there is no one-to-one relationship between wisdom and age. Some young people are wise
and some not; some older people are wise and some
not. This is a matter of individual endowment and
stance.

The setting for the first half of the book is that of
the Babylonian exile, beginning in 605 BC. The last
half seems to reflect a time after the death of Alex-
ander the Great (323 BC), when the Jews were

caught between the Ptolemies of Egypt and the Se-
leucids of Syria, suffering their heaviest persecution
under Antiochus Epiphanes (175-164 BC).[5] Most
scholars hold that the book took its present shape
under this second century BC crisis. Whatever the
date, just as Ezekiel should serve as a warning
against the presumptions of age, Daniel both affirms
youth and warns age.

In the interest of balance, it should be observed
that Daniel seems to have had a long ministry, beginning in 605 BC and traceable through the third year
of Cyrus (536 BC; see also 1:21; 10:1). This adds up to
about 70 years, his age being that plus whatever
were the years of his "youth" in 605 BC. That could
add up to 85 years or more. He did not retire at age
70! He was competent beyond age 70! Youth is affirmed in Daniel, but so is age.

Hosea

This powerful study (ca. 783-687 BC) of the unfaithfulness of Israel set forth by analogy of Gomer's
unfaithfulness to her husband, the prophet Hosea,
does not speak directly to the subject of age. It does
not intend to. What it intends to pursue, it does with
unsurpassed pathos and persuasiveness. To liken
Israel to a child (11:1) or refer to the happier days of
her youth (2:13) offers little to our study. The nearest approach to significance for the study of aging is
in 7:9, where Ephraim's gradual corruption by
aliens is likened to unnoticed aging: "Aliens devour
his strength, and he knows it not; gray hairs are
sprinkled upon him, and he knows it not." This is not
a comment on aging as such but a warning that
moral decay or defection from God can occur so
stealthily that one has little if any awareness of it.

People can *drift* from God just as they can deliberately rebel.

If 7:9 be applied to aging itself, some lessons are to be learned. It is not likely that in a literal sense one remains unaware of that sprinkling of gray hairs; if the mirror doesn't tell, some "friend" will point them out. Figuratively, "gray hairs" may sneak in without making their presence known. One may "age" beyond one's awareness of the fact. This may be harmless, or it may pose real problems for all concerned. Sometimes one's loss of capacity to cope or to function exceeds one's awareness of it (or willingness to acknowledge it). Others may be hurt or endangered in the process, as when an older person insists upon driving an automobile, even when the skill for it has dropped below the safety level. It may be on the job, where production or safety is threatened. It may be that the chief damage is to the older person's image when loss of capacity is apparent to all but the older person.

Here is where love needs its best wisdom and tact, both supportive and protective of one for whom "gray hairs are sprinkled upon him, and he knows it not." The public must be protected from the actions of older people who try to function beyond their capacities, even if at high risk to themselves and the public. Older people need to be protected from unduly endangering themselves and from unduly exposing their impairments when they are last to recognize their incapacities. Pulling this off without undue hurt to anyone is no easy assignment. As we grow older, it would help if we tried to keep ourselves open to the fact that impairments do come and they may reach a point where adjustments in life style must be made. Third parties who try to protect the public and the self-image of the aging need all the wisdom and love they can get for this high-risk ministry.

Joel

Joel, unknown outside this book, spoke to his nation devastated by locusts, probably in the fourth century BC (see 3:6). He begins with an appeal especially to the aged: "Hear this, you aged men, give ear, all inhabitants of the land!" (1:1). Consistently, he involves the whole nation, but here the "aged" have a special assignment. Their memory is the longest, and to them Joel appeals for a comparison of the current plight with any other in their lifetime. He sees the "aged" to have special responsibility in remembering, assessing, and telling (vv. 2-3).

Two references to "the elders" establish the fact that in the social/religious structure of Judaism in Joel's time were leaders known as "the elders." One responsibility of the elders had to do with the "solemn assembly": "Blow the trumpet in Zion; sanctify a fast; call a solemn assembly; gather the people. Sanctify the congregation; assemble the elders; gather the children, even nursing infants. Let the bridegroom leave his room, and the bride her chamber" (2:15-16). If the nation was to be restored, they needed to be brought together to hear God's word. It was to be inclusive of all people, of such priority that even bride and groom were to appear. From the oldest to the youngest, they were to gather. The elders probably were given heavy responsibility in bringing about such a "solemn assembly" (see 1:14).

The universalistic note sounded in 2:28-29 included "all flesh," that is, everybody. God promises the outpouring of his spirit upon male and female, old and young, and slaves. "Masters" are usually held to be included by implication, but Joel is silent here: "And it shall come to pass that I will pour out my spirit on all flesh; your sons and your daughters shall prophesy, your old men shall dream dreams, and your young men shall see visions. Even upon the menservants and maidservants in those days, I will pour out my spirit." Probably no real distinction is intended as to "dreams" and "visions," both related to divine revelation. There is no necessary implication that "old men" are mere dreamers or that "young men" are mere visionaries; for the intention is positive. Neither is it implied that the visions of the young are more positive or forward-looking than the dreams of the old. This is poetic parallelism, with youth and age equally affirmed. What is stressed is that old and young alike will receive God's Spirit. God's spirit is not restricted by sexual, legal, or calendar distinctions. Joel knows heavier responsibilities to fall upon "the elders," but privilege and blessing are intended universally.

Amos

This eighth century BC prophet is generally considered the first of the writing prophets. The book dates from about 750 BC or a little earlier. Amos' message came to him during the reign of Uzziah, king of Judah (783-742 BC) and Jereboam II, king of Israel (786-746 BC). Amos anticipated defeat and exile for Judah and Israel (2:4,6, and other scattered references), holding out hope only for a remnant (9:12). Scorning cultic or ritual performance, he demanded, "But let justice roll down like waters, and righteousness like an over-flowing stream" (5:24).

Amos was especially concerned for "the needy,"

"the poor," and "the afflicted" (1:6-7; 4:1; 5:11,12; 8:4,6). There is no reference to the aged. "Baldness on every head" (8:10) is a ritual act, not a matter of aging. The nearest approach to our subject is in the charge that "a man and his father go in to the same maiden" (2:7). When it comes to sin, there is no "generation gap," as father and son share the same prostitute. Otherwise, the book has nothing to offer on the subject of age or aging. It could be that age posed no problem in the world Amos surveyed. It could be that the problems were there, but the issue had not surfaced. Speculation here is precarious. Amos gives us more on other subjects than we yet have really taken into our practicing religion. From others we may be instructed in matters of age and aging.

Obadiah

There are only 21 verses in this book, a scathing denunciation of Edom for gloating over the fall of Jerusalem (586 BC). Unless "the wise men out of Edom" (v. 8) are understood as aged, which is not explicit or necessarily implied, there is nothing in the book bearing on our subject. Noted for wisdom, Edom's insensitivity to human misery, even for her kin, attests to her loss of wisdom, whatever the age of her "wise men."

Jonah

The Book of Jonah seems to date from the fourth century BC, reflecting the time of Ezra-Nehemiah. It was a time when Jewish particularism as represented by the priestly power structure was rampant and rigid, excluding aliens in the name of purity of race.[6] Over against this perspective is the Book of

Jonah, a book of unsurpassed power in its portrayal of God's universal concern. The prophet Jonah *wanted* Nineveh destroyed; God wanted Nineveh to repent and be saved. Jonah pitied himself in the guise of pitying a gourd plant from which he sought shade from a blazing sun; God pitied Nineveh (4:9-10).

Like the "cracker" on a whip, the book's final verse may be its most stinging: "And should not I pity Nineveh, that great city, in which there are more than a hundred and twenty thousand persons who do not know their right hand from their left, and also much cattle?" (4:11). Those who "do not know their right hand from their left" may be infants, but probably the reference is a figurative one to all persons (*'adam*) in Nineveh, bewildered "pagans" who are lost to God and the quality of life he wills for all people.[7] This would include young and old alike. The Book of Jonah does not mention the aged, but its impassioned concern for all people compels enlightened conscience to seek out all the "Ninevites" so easily ignored or despised by "piety" but so precious to God. In the compassionate perspective and commitment of the Book of Jonah is not only a true revelation of the love of God for all people but the best security for any "who do not know their right hand from their left," whether young or old.

Micah

Micah probably was the last of the four great eighth century BC prophets, preceded by Amos, Hosea, and Isaiah. The word of the Lord came to him during the reigns of Jotham, Ahaz, and Hezekiah, kings of Judah (739-693 BC), and he directed his message primarily to Samaria and Jerusalem (1:1).

Micah found "none upright among men" (7:2), but he held the capital cities of Samaria and Jerusalem primarily responsible for the moral failure of Israel and Judah and he placed heaviest guilt upon such leaders as princes, priests, prophets, and judges (3:1,9,11; 4:9; 7:3). He did not single out the aged for failure, but the kings and counselors who failed the people, the judges who were bribed, the priests who were hired, and the prophets who divined for money were not all young men. The people were not guilt-less, but they suffered unduly through the defaults and failures of the leaders who misled. Although Micah was not directly concerned with the "genera-tion gap," he did in passing censure such disrespect and disservice as when "the son treats the father with contempt, the daughter rises up against her mother" (7:6).

Micah's legacy includes one of the Bible's great encapsulizations of authentic religion: "He has showed you, O man, what is good; and what does the Lord require of you but to do justice, and to love kindness, and to walk humbly with your God?" (6:8). Young and old are secure when religion moves re-sponsibly in that direction.

Nahum

The book of Nahum is poetic, written possibly as liturgy about the time of the fall of Nineveh to the Babylonians and Medes in 612 BC and directed against Nineveh. The book is difficult both for Jew-ish and Christian conscience, as it can be understood as almost exclusively particularistic and vindictive. In the book, pent-up feelings find expression; but it may not take too much liberty to say with one inter-preter, "Nahum's voice is the voice of tortured and outraged humanity."[8] Nahum spoke out bitterly against the brutality of Nineveh, and this may capture the feeling of many across the ages who have suffered under man's inhumanity to man. Seventh century BC Assyria, of which Nineveh was the capital, was grossly brutal, not only as attested by other nations but by her own art. Gouging out eyes, hacking off hands, mutilating women and men in various ways, and putting captives to torture were atrocities not only practiced but boasted of by ancient Assyria.[9] However assessed otherwise, Nahum does cry out against such dehumanizing practice.

There is nothing in the book bearing explicitly upon the subject of age and aging. We can draw nothing from this book on our subject except that dehumanizing in whatever form or at whatever time is to be protested and resisted, even as in Nahum. No age group escapes the dehumanizing practices of "humanity," and old people have their own vulnerability to such practice. Some old people today are actually subjected to physical abuse by their kin. Many more suffer in more subtle ways, robbed of their dignity nonetheless.

Habakkuk

There is no explicit reference in this book to age or aging, and probably nothing implicit. Habakkuk, like Nahum, addressed the situation under which the Chaldeans (Babylon) defeated Assyria (605 BC) and extended her dominion over many nations, including Judah. Whereas Nahum turned his wrath upon Nineveh, Habakkuk struggled with the more complex problem of both Judah's sin, on the one hand, and the ruthless aggression of Babylon on the other.[10] Habakkuk struggled with the problem of the suffering of righteous people and the outward triumphs of the wicked. This is the problem of relating a good God to an evil world, with the aching question, Why?[11] Upon receiving the answer that God was using Babylon as an instrument by which he disciplined Judah, Habakkuk responded with yet more agony as to why one nation would be punished by a nation even less righteous (1:12-17).

The final resolution for Habakkuk was in the assurance of ultimate reversals for the wicked and the righteous. For the wicked there comes ultimately the self-destruction which is inherent in evil. For the righteous there is ultimate vindication. Habakkuk concludes: "Behold, he whose soul is not upright in him shall fail, but the righteous shall live by his faith" (2:4). "His faith" could be rendered "his faithfulness." "His" may refer to man or God. Probably the intention is, "A person will live by remaining faithful to God." The idea may be, "A person lives by faith in the faithfulness of God."

At best, life is hard for young and old in every generation. More needs to be said to and done for young and old, but basic to coping meaningfully with life is Habakkuk's assurance—life for the righteous does have meaning now, and in remaining faithful to the God who remains faithful to us, there are both meaning now and victory ahead.

Zephaniah

Only in 1:1 is direct identification of Zephaniah offered. He was the great-great-grandson of "Hezekiah," and the word of the Lord came to him "in the days of Josiah the son of Amon, king of Judah." If

"Hezekiah" is the reforming king of Judah (715-687 BC), then Zephaniah was in the royal line. Since Josiah reigned in 640-609 BC, Zephaniah is by some thought to have been a very young man when he uttered his prophecy, if indeed his great-great-grandfather was the King Hezekiah. Neither the royal descent nor the youth of the prophet is established. If either or both are correct, some reflection on Zephaniah's perspective and tone may be in order as it bears upon the factor of age. The hazards here are fully acknowledged.

Whether of royal line and/or young, Zephaniah is a prophet of doom, holding out hope for but a remnant in Judah, with none for the larger world. He opens with a picture of God who "will utterly sweep away everything from the face of the earth" (1:2). "The great day of the Lord" is seen as "near," "bitter," and a day of "wrath," "distress and anguish," "ruin and devastation," "darkness and gloom," and "clouds and thick darkness" (2:14-16). There is no expressed concern for the privations and burdens of the common man. There is what some see in the prophets as a "puritanical" spirit. It by no means follows that such perspective and tone could come only from a youth who grew up in a sheltered, royal line, for there are many old men found with the same stance and spirit. It does follow, whatever the age and/or status of Zephaniah, that aging should heighten sensitivity to the little people who get caught in the crunch and mellow the spirit even where the call to repentance remains uncompromised. Whether the Book of Zephaniah is the proper base for it or not, it follows that a sinful and suffering world needs the gifts of both youth and age in its prophetic voices.

Haggai

Haggai's one mission, so far as our information goes, was the practical one of getting the Temple in Jerusalem rebuilt. Sixteen years had gone by, and it had been all talk and no results. Haggai saw both prosperity and piety to be tied up with the rebuilding of the Temple. It is generally agreed that he was a realist who could get things done. He was a leader who could motivate and activate people. He was a man of energy and drive.

Our interest in Haggai relates to speculations as to his age, as in the case of Zephaniah unestablished but with some possible clue. Some see in 2:3 the implication that Haggai was an old man, among those who could remember the former Temple: "Who is left among you that saw this house in its former glory? How do you see it now? Is it not in your sight as nothing?" Obviously, the passage is at most a clue and not a proof. As far as it goes, it implies age more so than youth.

Our complaint is with those who have presumed to settle the question of Haggai's age by the qualities of his work. John Patterson is representative of the stereotype: "In view of the energy displayed in the drive to rebuild the temple, we would imagine him to be in the prime of life; the qualities which he reveals are not usually found in old men."[12] This is a *non sequitur.* This is stereotype without defense. There is no fixed age in which one reaches "the prime of life." Some people never have much energy or drive or power to motivate and activate others. It is not uncommon to find these qualities in old people (for example, Winston Churchill, Franklin Roosevelt, David Ben-Gurion, Golda Meir, and others). Haggai's age remains an unsettled question, and it is false to argue backward from his manner. It does not follow that age itself determines competence or "capacity for getting things done." Young and old are entitled to individual assessment, not the victims of stereotype.

Zechariah

In Zechariah's description of a restored and cleansed Jerusalem, against the background of its Exilic ruin, God will again dwell in the midst of Jerusalem, and Jerusalem is to be called "the faithful city" (8:3). Then follows one of the most beautiful passages in Scripture bearing on our subject of age: "Thus says the Lord of hosts: Old men and old women shall again sit in the streets of Jerusalem, each with staff in hand for every age. And the streets of the city shall be full of boys and girls, playing in the streets" (vv. 4-5). Aged men and women with their walking sticks and little children playing in the streets! This picture of the "extended family" is in itself beautiful enough. But there is more. This is the ideal city, the holy city from which much "piety" in ancient times banned the blind, the lame, and anyone with any physical impairment. Zechariah makes room in the center of life in the Holy City for people like the aged. One does not have to have sturdy legs and twenty-twenty vision to qualify to walk openly in the streets of Jerusalem, "the faithful city."

In striking contrast is the Temple Scroll of the Qumran Community (one of the Dead Sea Scrolls), in its exclusion from the Temple-city of any found with "impurity" or impairment as judged by its holiness code. The War Scroll describes an expected holy war between "the sons of light" (the Qumranites) and "the sons of darkness" (Romans), and from their war camps were to be excluded boys, women, and lame, blind, crippled, those with bodily blemishes or impurities (VII, 5-5).[13] According to Jacob Milgrom, the Temple Scroll (45-12-14) applied the same restrictions to the Temple-city.[14]

Zechariah is linked with Haggai, both having concentrated their efforts at getting the Temple rebuilt following the Exile (Ezra 5:1-2; 6:14-15; Neh. 12:16). They began their prophecies in 520 BC. Zechariah is thought by some to have been a young man (see Patterson, p. 227, following Sellin), this dependent upon "that young man" of 2:4 being Zechariah himself. John D. W. Watts follows L. G. Rignell in so understanding the reference.[15] This may well follow, but Calkins falls into stereotype in saying, "Like Zephaniah, he was a young man. But while Zephaniah represents the melancholy of youth, Zechariah exhibits its optimism."[16] Melancholy and optimism are no more qualities of youth than they are of old age. They are individual moods, not directly correlated to age. As observed recurrently, aging should be on the side of mellowness, but it may do little or nothing in that respect or even worsen one's mood. Direction, not driving time of itself, determines the destination.

Malachi

This book probably was written about 460 BC, in the time of Ezra and Nehemiah but after Haggai and Zechariah, for the Temple was again in use and already suffering abuse. For our purpose, the chief relevance probably is to be found in the recurrence of the father/son or father/children motif (1:2,6; 2:10; 4:6). The term "father" is used as a role model for God, and it appears in a literal sense in the family relationship.

The first affirmation of the book is basic: " 'I have loved you,' says the Lord" (1:2). God affirms his love for Israel. Next, God is portrayed as a "father," with the reminder that "A son honors his father" (v. 6). The point is that Israel should honor God as any Israelite knew a son should honor his father. Assumed is just that, that a proper son honors his father. The son/father relationship is not strictly a youth/aged person relationship, for many fathers are themselves young people, from the teens upwards in age. At least the age factor is there because it is inherent in the relationship that the father is older than his child. What Malachi assumes and prescribes, then, a son's honoring his father, has some implication for the matter of youth's honoring age.

Many today shrink back from reference to God as "father." Some do so because many modern fathers are poor models for God. To many children, a father is that man who comes home drunk and beats up the family. Obviously the model does not communicate well there. With a new sensitivity to the rightful personhood of woman, others find the biblical term sexist when applied to God. Whatever the most serviceable terminology today, in Malachi's day neither problem had surfaced. "Father" stood for something positive in the Jewish world. As to the other issue, "Father" is even in biblical usage a model; and it does not imply that God is male. In Genesis 1:27, male and female are created together and both in the image of God. This is not to say that God is male or female, but it does imply that both male and female answer to something in God. This is not the burden of this present study on age and aging, but if "father" constitutes only an interference word, it defeats our purpose (see Evelyn and Frank Stagg, *Woman in the World of Jesus*, Westminster, 1978, for biblical and other perspectives on woman).

A second principle with relevance to age is found in 2:10, "Have we not all one father? Has not one God created us? Why then are we faithless to one another, profaning the covenant of our fathers?" Age is not the subject here, but human relationship is. If God is one, here viewed under the model of "father," it follows that we should relate to one another as brothers and sisters. We are intended to be one family under God and a people bound together under covenant. This calls for mutual respect. True, Malachi reduces this in context to a requirement of marriage only within Israel; but the principle lends itself to a wider application to all human relationships. Although age is not mentioned, under one God as "Father" age-group relationships, along with all other relationships, find their rightful standard.

The very last verse of Malachi is significant: "And he will turn the hearts of the fathers to their children and the hearts of the children to their fathers, lest I come and smite the land with a curse" (4:6). Again, father/child is not identical with youth/age, but the principle of mutual and affectionate affirmation holds for both.

5

Age in the Synoptic
Gospels and Acts

For a century and a half the close relationship of Matthew, Mark, and Luke has been recognized; and these three Gospels are known as Synoptic, that is, basically one in perspective. It is not that simple, and the relationship of these three Gospels is yet a puzzle to scholars, but they have so much in common that they may be considered together here. It is generally recognized that the Gospel of Luke and the book of Acts are not only by one author but two volumes on a continuing theme, often designated Luke-Acts. Hence the grouping of these four writings in this chapter.

There is considerable evidence in the Synoptic Gospels and Acts with significant bearing upon age and aging, even though the subject is never pursued in its own right. There is frequent attention to age, but the pros and cons of age and aging are never discussed as such. Whether a subject neglected or a subject then requiring no special attention may be debated. In any event, the Synoptics and Acts are rewarding studies for our subject.

Any apparent neglect of age, aging, or agism in these writings is not due to indifference or inattention to human need, for they give major attention to the priority of the personal over all else. The personal in relationship—God, you, and neighbor—is what matters most with Jesus and with those closest to his concerns. Jesus was concerned for all people, and he was concerned for each person at each level of need. These concerns of Jesus so dominate the text that proof-texting is almost redundant. To fail to see this is to miss the thrust of the Gospels. One may conclude that either there was no discrimination against age calling for special attention or that concern for the aged is implied in Jesus' concern for all people, especially for the disfranchised, the neglected, the disadvantaged, and the rejected. Many such are singled out for explicit attention, and probably more explicit attention was not given to older people because in Jewish piety there was great respect for age.

Sensitivity to human need appears throughout the Synoptics and Acts, with special attention to the disadvantaged or neglected: non-Jews, Jews considered "unclean" by piety, the physically sick and impaired, the emotionally and psychologically disturbed, women, the poor, the sinful, and all suffering under discrimination. Jesus offered inclusion on a basis within the reach of any: "Whoever does the will of God is my brother and sister and mother" (Mark 3:35; see also Matt. 12:50; Luke 8:21). Luke-Acts devotes major attention to the inclusion of the excluded in the family of God, as the Gospel is preached "unhindered" (Acts 28:31) to any who will hear, Jew or Gentile, from Jerusalem to Rome. Jesus gave special attention to the poor, the captives, the blind, and the oppressed in his inaugural sermon at Nazareth, as he interpreted the thrust of his mission (Luke 4:16-30). Replying to the searching question of John the Baptist, "Are you the Coming One or should we await another?" (Luke 7:19),

Jesus pointed to his ministry to the blind, the lame, the lepers, the deaf, the poor, the sick, and the dead (vv. 21-22). In his most graphic description of the final judgment, Jesus stressed attention to the hungry, the thirsty, the stranger, the naked, the sick, and the imprisoned as decisive (Matt. 25:31-46).

With all this attention to human need, why is there not more direct attention to the needs of the aged? Even in the anticipated sufferings under the destruction of Jerusalem, special pity is expressed for pregnant women and mothers nursing their babies (Mark 13:17; see also Matt. 24:19; Luke 21:23); but no mention is made of old people and the special hardships upon them as they are forced to flee their homes. Were there traces of "agism" or discrimination against older people, such silence would be significant. Because such negative notes are absent from the Synoptics and Acts and because there are positive affirmations of both young and old, as well as censure of each on occasion, caution is best exercised in assessing such silence.

The best clue to what we find and do not find probably derives from the situation. There was overt discrimination against aliens, women, the poor, the physically and emotionally ill, and those not complying with cultic codes like Sabbath observance and keeping a distance from what was called "unclean"; and these discriminations and injustices are protested in the Synoptics and Acts, with a clear call to rectifying these injustices. Why equal attention is not given to older people is not apparent, but there is nothing to imply deliberate inattention. There is no negative attitude toward age in these writings.

The prominence of "the elders" in both Judaism and the emerging church is significant, as attested throughout the Synoptics and Acts. Uniformly, "the elders" are included at the highest level of authority in Judaism of this period, and "the elders" are among the recognized authorities in the churches at Jerusalem, Ephesus, and elsewhere (see Acts 11:30; 14:23; 15:4,6,22,23; 20:17; 21:18). In Judaism, "the elders" are cited along with the high priests and other rulers of the Jews, "the elders of the Council" and simply "the elders" or "the Council" designating the same ruling body (see Mark 8:31; 11:27; 14:53; 15:1; Matt. 15:2; 26:3,57; 27:1; 28:12; Luke 20:1; 22:66; Acts 4:5,8,23; 22:5,30; 23:14-15; 24:1; 25:15). Clearly, older men were given prominent and powerful positions in the government of both Jewish and early Christian people.

It is true as already noted that "elder" came to designate a ruling class with a lessening of emphasis upon age as such, just as is true for "senator" or "senate." Although the range in age for "the elders" may have been wide, even the term is significant. "Elders" originally were actually older persons, and whatever the lowering of age eligibility, there is nothing to imply a lessening of respect for seniority at the ruling level. Early Christians seem to have followed the Jewish pattern in looking to "the elders" for wisdom and justice at the decision-making level.

In the Synoptics and Acts it is equally clear that the character of "the elders" is not guaranteed by virtue of age. The Jewish elders appear almost always in a bad light. This is not charged to their age, there being no implication that their judgment was impaired with advancing age or that they became less just with aging. Rather it is the "establishment" mentality of the "elders of the Council" which best accounts for the negative way in which they are

seen in the Synoptics and Acts. Jesus' chief opposi-
tion came from the "establishment," especially the
Pharisees and Sadducees who saw their vested interests as threatened by the manner and teachings of
Jesus. Jesus' sharpest conflicts were with the Pharisees, the Sadducees, the high priests, and "the elders." If there is a lesson here, it is not that "You
can't trust a person beyond thirty (or whatever)"; it
is that we tend to defend our vested interests. The
"ins" resist the "outs," and "the establishment" re-
sists reform or the rising class. One may have an
"establishment" stance whatever one's age.

That there is no prejudice against the aged in the
Synoptics or Acts appears not only from the absence
of any overt "agism" but from the strength and
beauty ascribed to certain old people, especially in
Luke 1—2. Luke begins his two volumes with a picture of the Jewish piety out of which John the Baptist and Jesus came. The picture is beautiful.
Throughout these two chapters is a sense of the
presence of God, worship, thanksgiving, trust in the
goodness of God, hope for redemption from sin and
from whatever holds people in bondage. Much of
these two chapters is poetic and hymnic. Old people
are featured throughout, except for the virgin Mary
and the child Jesus.

Zechariah and Elizabeth, from whom John the
Baptist came, "both were advanced in years" (Luke
1:7). Zechariah expressed it thus: "I am an old man,
and my wife is advanced in years" (1:18). Precisely
how old they were is not disclosed, but they were
seen as beyond the years where they normally could
become parents. Elizabeth was "in her old age"
(1:30). The conception of a child in their old age was
ascribed to a miracle of God, but Zechariah's func-

tioning as a priest at the temple is narrated as something not calling for explanation: "He was serving as priest before God" (1:8). Although "advanced in years," he remained active. He had not been retired. Offering the incense at the altar of prayer in the temple was a once-in-a-lifetime honor for a priest, and Zechariah was entrusted with this high responsibility though "advanced in years."

Simeon's age is not specified, but presumably he was an old man. Seeing the promised Messiah was the last goal of his life, and for that he had awaited (2:26). When he took the child Jesus into his arms, he declared his readiness to die: "Lord, now let thou thy servant depart in peace, according to thy word; for my eyes have seen thy salvation" (2:29-30). The tone of the passage implies that Simeon was an old man. He is presented as a model in faith, hope, and piety.

Anna's age was not less than 84 years when she celebrated the coming of Jesus as "the redemption of Jerusalem" (2:36-38). Anna was a prophetess, described thus: "advanced in many days, having lived with a husband seven years from her virginity, and being a widow up to eighty-four years." The Greek syntax is not clear as to the point from which the 84 years are counted, whether from her birth or widowhood. In any event, Anna was at least 84 years old, and she was active and alert in her long vigil at the temple. Both a woman and aged, she occupied a central place in the piety of Judaism and the emerging church.

Interestingly, Luke's opening chapters feature the four old people named above (Zechariah, Elizabeth, Simeon, Anna) and two young people, Mary and the child Jesus. Mary's age is not given, but youth is implied. Jesus appears first as the newborn child and then at age 12 (2:41-52). Of course, Mary and Jesus are exceptional or even unique. They are not presented in a good light because they are young, but here youth does appear in good light. In fact, the four aged persons and the two young persons are presented positively. They are not good and beautiful because they are old or young, but old and young can thus be good and beautiful. There is no "agism" here. There is no stereotype here. Each character in this beautiful introduction to Luke-Acts is treated as an individual. Their beautiful qualities are not determined by age but by their own personhood in relationship with God and other people.

Only by superficial reading of the Synoptics and Acts may one find the stereotype of agism. Careful reading discloses the fact that older people can be good or bad, and so can young people. Already observed is the fact that "the elders of the Council" are prevailingly seen in a bad light, not because of their age but because of their "establishment" stance. Young people are more often presented in a good light, but not always. The strongest affirmation of youth is in Jesus' holding children as a model in discipleship. He took little children into his arms, blessed them, and said, "Truly I say to you, whoever does not receive the kingdom of God as a child, shall not enter into it" (Mark 10:13-16; see also Matt. 19:13-15; Luke 18:15-17). Childlike qualities are the ones required, presumably like those of trust and pliability. This is not to imply that all children are good and old age bad. It does recognize that it is childlike to trust and to be teachable and that with aging is the danger if not the tendency to become fixed in one's ways. It is not to be overlooked that "childlikeness" can be lost early in life, for many young people have closed minds and fixed ways. Neither is it to be forgotten that Jesus warned against being "childish," like little children displeased with whatever is offered them (Matt. 11:16-19). Children can be "childlike" or "childish," and so may adults. Calendar age alone does not determine whether we are open or closed to truth or more meaningful life.

Young people appear both positively and negatively in the Synoptics. In Mark is the strange story about "a young man" who was following Jesus after his arrest and who, upon being seized, left his linen cloth in the hands of his would-be captors and fled naked (14:51-52)! No explanation is given for the inclusion of this remarkable story in this Gospel. It may be autobiographical, the young man having been Mark himself. Probably it intends to dramatize the failure of Jesus' disciples, for in the Gospel of Mark only the shepherd is fully faithful, the flock is scattered in fear and disarray (14:27-31,51; 16:7). The disciples compete for honors and power, make great boasts and promises, betray, lie, and flee. The women fare better, but they too fear and tremble (16:8). Probably the story of the youth who fled naked is included to dramatize the failure of the disciples, not to single out youth for judgment.

Significantly, Mark features "a young man" in the closing chapter, at the empty tomb (16:5). The role of this young man is positive, for he proclaims to the women the fact of the resurrection and the further commissioning of the women to proclaim the good news to the apostles. It may be that there is a deliberate linkage between stories of the two young men, one negative and one positive. The stories may dramatize both failure and restoration in discipleship. In any event, youth is presented both ways, with no implication of stereotype for youth or age. Failure may come at any age and so may redemption.

In one of his parables, Jesus portrayed "a young man" as failing, clinging to his wealth and turning from eternal life (Matt. 19:16-22). He did not fail because he was young but because he was in the clutches of his wealth, a fate to which old and young alike are vulnerable.

In Acts, the church had some known as "the young men" (5:6,10). These appear positively, although little is disclosed about them. Their selection as pall bearers for Ananias and Sapphira may have been related to their physical strength as young men. That being young does not guarantee goodness is illustrated in the case of Saul of Tarsus, "a young man" when he engaged in fanatical zeal even to the point of approving the stoning of Stephen and dragging men and women out of their houses to flog or jail them (Acts 7:58; 8:3; 9:1-2). Being young did not make Saul immune to an "establishment" stance, even to its extreme. Eutychus was "a young man" (Acts 20:9) who went to sleep during Paul's long sermon and fell out of a window. Sleeping through a sermon is not exclusive to old or young. Paul's sister's son was "a young man" when he showed not only family loyalty but courage in exposing a plot to take Paul's life (Acts 23:17-22). Courage is found in some old and in some young people, and it is absent from some old and some young people.

In Peter's sermon on the Day of Pentecost, the perspective is egalitarian in the picture cited from Joel in which God's Spirit is poured out upon "all flesh," young and old, male and female (Acts

2:17-18). This indiscriminate outpouring of God's Spirit includes sons and daughters, young men and old men, manservants and maidservants. Some distinction may be implied in that young men will "see visions" and old men "dream dreams," but probably the distinction is only in imagery with no substantive distinction intended. This is poetic parallelism, with imagery in terms of vision and imagination. "Dreaming dreams" here is not looking back but looking forward. Old men here are not represented as living in the past; they, along with the young, look ahead to the ideal, whether in "vision" or "dream." The citation is from the prophet Joel, but the non-discriminating perspective is in keeping with that of Luke-Acts as a whole.

To conclude, the Synoptic Gospels and Acts do not discuss the pros and cons of age or aging as such, but important lessons are found in these writings. Agism does not appear in these writings. There is no prejudice nor stereotype. The prominence of "the elders" in both Judaism and the early church reflects both custom and the expectation that wisdom should be found in older people. With this is the clear recognition that elders may be good or bad. So also may young people be good or bad, opened or closed in mind. Personal qualities, positive and negative, depend ultimately upon factors beyond age itself.

6
Age in the Johannine Writings

Five New Testament writings are traditionally associated with John, usually thought of as one of the sons of Zebedee. The question of authorship and the relationship of these five writings to one another are unsolved problems in New Testament scholarship, and it is beyond the scope of this book even to attempt a solution. The grouping of these books is not merely arbitrary, and there is evidence for at least a "Johannine School"[1] behind these writings. Their diversity and commonality give support to this theory. In this chapter we will consider the questions of age and aging in the Gospel of John, the three letters attributed to John, and the book of Revelation.

The Gospel of John

One major passage in the Gospel of John opens the door to a consideration of the character of age or aging. Nicodemus posed the question, "How can a man be born when he is old?" (3:4). This was in response to Jesus' claim, "Truly, truly, I say to you, except one be begotten from above he cannot see the kingdom of God" (v. 3). As usual in this Gospel, meaning moves at two levels, the surface or literal and a deeper level. Of course, Jesus was calling not for a literal return to the womb and a second physical birth; he was calling for such a radical break with the past that it would be like being "born anew" or, probably, being "begotten from above." Jesus called this mature man to a fresh start in life, marked by radically new perspective and commitment. That Nicodemus struggled for understanding does not obscure the significant fact that Jesus recognized in him, an adult of some years, the possibility of such a new birth.

There is a widely held view that openness to change diminishes with age. An old proverb has it, "You can't teach an old dog new tricks." It is incontestible that persistence in a certain way tends to confirm one in it, and one can become "sot in one's ways." But the passage before us does not see openness to change to be the art of the young alone. True, Nicodemus does not see how one can reenter the womb, and he may also resist the idea that the old can change radically. Whatever the perspective of Nicodemus, it is not the perspective ascribed here to Jesus that the old cannot change. Jesus sees Nicodemus as redeemable. He can be "born anew," or better, be "begotten from above."

Physical impairments, like arteriosclerosis, may render one beyond significant change; and one may so refuse the light that one's sight goes out (see John 9:34); but age as such does not constitute a point of no return. Old people can learn, and they can find new direction and new meaning for life. Nicodemus was called to decision, not abandoned to a fate imposed by age. Closed minds are found in people of all ages, and so are open minds. There are young people who have never opened their minds to anything outside their traditions. Simplistic and dogmatic answers are mouthed by young and old, just as investigative and creative minds are found in both young and old. Jesus does not ask, "How old are you?" but "Are you willing to see?" Significantly, he asked a man lame for thirty-eight years, "Do you wish to be made whole?" (5:6). He gave sight to a man born blind (9:4-7). He declared that he had come into the world "that those who do not see may see, and that those who see may become blind" (9:39). From the context, it appears that Jesus meant that he could and would give spiritual sight to those willing to receive it, but that he would impose it upon none. In fact, to refuse the light results ultimately in the loss of the power to see. The Pharisees who condemned Jesus for healing a blind man on the sabbath remained "blind" not because they were old but because they refused to see. They rejected the offered light. Again, age as such is not the decisive factor in "birth from above" or in becoming able "to see."

At this point and throughout this book it is important to distinguish between voluntary and involuntary factors in human condition or behavior. Purely physiological factors can render older people beyond the capacity for responsible action or change. Likewise, purely physical factors can render a baby or child unable to function responsibly. In such cases it is as cruel and dehumanizing (more to the guilty than the designated victim) to make little jokes about "senility" as about retardation. On the other hand, there are voluntary factors in "blindness" or resistance to new and more meaningful existence. Young and old are vulnerable to such voluntary rejection of "birth from above" or "light" sent from God. Nicodemus in chapter 3 and the Pharisees in chapter 9 stood before challenging new options, and factors other than age were decisive.

The Letters of John

First John is anonymous, but the writer appears to be an old man. He addresses his readers as his "little children" (2:1,12-13,18; 3:7,18; 4:4; 5:21). In one passage he addresses "little children," "young men," and "fathers" (2:12-14). He speaks often of "that which was from the beginning" (1:1; 2:7, 13-14,24; 3:8,11; see also 2 John 5-6). These evidences are not decisive, but they seem to imply seniority. Tradition has it that John was an old man when he wrote. This likewise is indecisive.

The writer of 2 and 3 John identifies himself as "the elder." Whether the term implies age or office is indecisive. As seen already, the term originally implied age and then came to designate persons to whom certain authority and responsibility were given. Although actual age came later to be secondary to being an "elder," in the early church "elders" probably were older people. If the three letters before us do come from the same person, the cumulative force favors his being an older man.

If John was an old man, his powers were not diminished. His concern for the past does not imply that he was living in the past. His writing is filled with concern for the present and for the future. He calls for responsible living in the present, with emphasis upon light, life, and love. Light and darkness are moral terms to him, and his call is away from darkness and into light. He calls not only for righteous living but for sensitivity to the daily needs of people around us (1 John 3:16-18). John does not idealize the past and despair of the future; rather he sees that "the darkness is passing away and the true

light is already shining" (1 John 2:8). John not only
reaches back to that which is "from the beginning,"
but he anticipates an even greater future: "Beloved,
now are we God's children, and not yet does it appear what we shall be; for we know that if he be
manifested, we shall be like him, for we shall see him
just as he is" (3:2).

It is from 2 John that it becomes clear why the
writer keeps harking back to "that which was from
the beginning." There were those who saw themselves as the progressives and who lived only for a
future uninformed by the past: "Everyone going
forward and not abiding in the teaching of Christ is
without God" (2 John 9). These seem to be self-
styled "spiritual" people who have gone beyond
Christ. Probably they are Gnostics who find Jesus
too earthly. They go with "the Spirit." John calls
them back to the historical Jesus, to "that which
was from the beginning." John's opponents try to
lay claim to the future without holding on to the
past. John keeps the balance between past, present,
and future. He is not locked into the past, but
neither does he find history to be "bunk." He draws
upon the past for instruction for the present and the
future. He is open to past, present, and future, each
in its proper place.

Whether young or old, John avoids the sacrificing
of the past to the future or the future to the past. He
avoids the emptying of the present by living only in
the past or only for the future. He well may have
been an old man when he wrote with such power
about the past, present, and future. Such balance is
not the exclusive possession of young or old. Aging
should be on the side of such balance.

In 1 John 2:12-14 are some intriguing lines addressed to "children," "fathers," and "young men." Each group is commended for certain characteristics and achievements. It is possible to derive stereotype or even agism from the passage, if it is treated mechanically. The passage is highly poetic, and must be read with imagination and not mechanically or slavishly. Some variations in the passage may be simply stylistic and not intended to be pressed unduly. For example, the present tense is used three times in verses 12-13 ("I write"), and the aorist tense is used three times in verse 14 ("I wrote," or possibly another way of saying "I write). The context does not seem to imply a literal distinction between present and past writing (the aorist tense can cover any kind of action).[2]

In the light of the above, it is precarious to read too much into age distinctions in the passage. In 2:1 all the readers are addressed as his "little children" (teknia). It is not probable that in 2:12 only the literally young (teknia) have had their sins forgiven. There could be some point to the writer's saying of the "fathers" that they know "the one from the beginning," yet all Christians know Christ. Older people may know some things from the past not known to younger people, but old and young alike may know directly him who is from the beginning. Young men are commended because they have conquered "the evil one" (v. 13), because they are "strong," and because the word of God abides in them (v. 14). There may be some implication that temptation comes especially to the young, but there is no age which does not have its temptations. Probably the age distinctions are not to be pressed here, the variations in terms as in style serving the dramatic purposes of poetry rather than the pedantry

of literalism. The passage is offered in all serious-
ness, with encouragement to all for a triumphant life
in Christ.

First John 5:1 may contain an insight with power
more explosive than may appear to casual reading.
The point of the passage is that those who trust
Jesus as the Christ are children of God, and one who
loves God will also love God's children. A close translation is as follows: "Everyone trusting that Jesus is
the Christ has been begotten out of God, and everyone loving the one who has begotten loves the one
having been begotten out of him." This means that
if we love God we will love any child of God. Many
modern translations find here a reference to every
parent/child relationship; that is, to love the parent is
to love the child. The Revised Standard Version
renders it: "and everyone who loves the parent loves
the child" (5b). *Today's English Version* has it, "and
whoever loves a father loves also his child." *The
New English Bible* has it, "and to love the parent
means to love his child." This probably goes beyond
the intention of the text. Older translations probably
had it right to begin with, seeing the meaning to be
that to love God is to love his child (see KJV; C. B.
Williams). John has the family of God in mind, and to
him loving God and loving his children go together.

Modern translations probably go beyond the intention of 5:1, but ideally love of parents and love of
children should go together. There is no proper place
for competitiveness here. It would be great if to love
the parents meant always to love the children and
vice versa. Unfortunately, this does not follow. If
what we call love were really the love about which
John wrote, it would follow that none would be ex-

cluded, for that love discriminates against neither young nor old.

The Book of Revelation

There is no trace of deliberate agism in Revelation, certainly no stereotype or prejudice against any age group. If a case may be made for preferential treatment of any age group, it would be favorable to older persons. There is no denigration of youth, but there are some positive affirmations of age, whatever the motive and whether deliberate or not.

In the awesome vision of the risen Christ walking among his churches (1:9-20), he appears with at least some of the markings generally associated with age: "His head and his hair were white as wool, as white as snow" (v. 14). No hint is given as to the meaning of the symbolism or it significance. White hair may appear in youth, but normally it is associated with age. White may symbolize purity, but there is no hint that here it bears that symbolic intention. Probably the whiteness here of head and hair serves as a linkage with him who is "the Ancient of Days" in Daniel 7:9-14, from which passage Revelation draws in its portrayal of the risen Christ. In Daniel "the Ancient of Days" is God before whom stands "One like a Son of Man" (7:13). Daniel says of the Ancient of Days, "His vesture was like snow, and the hair of his head like pure wool" (v. 9). In Revelation the one "like a Son of Man" is Christ, and he bears striking resemblance to "the Ancient of Days," in particular with his whiteness of head and hair. Probably here, as throughout the New Testament, the balance is maintained between the divine identity and the dis-

tinction between the eternal God and Jesus as the
Christ. The deity is clearly affirmed, and so is the
humanity. To see the Son is to see the Father (John
10:30; 14:9), yet the Father is greater than the Son
(John 14:28). God himself is uniquely present in
Jesus Christ (see John 1:1,14; 2 Cor. 5:19), but God
was before the incarnation and God is greater than
and more than appears in any revelation he gives of
himself. The limitation is not with God but with us;
we can never encompass God. God is always more
than we encounter or know. This is the tension implied in the Gospel of John, where to see the Son is to
see the Father, yet the Father is greater than the
Son. God is greater than his appearance, even when
"the Word" becomes "flesh."

Probably it is this tension which is embedded in
Revelation 1:10-16. Revelation preserves the distinction of Daniel between "the Ancient of Days" and
"One like a Son of Man" who appeared before him.
Revelation also affirms the essential identity between the risen Christ and the eternal God, ascribing here to Christ some of the symbolism which in
Daniel applies to the Ancient of Days. In Revelation
1:8 it is God, the Almighty, the eternal one, who is
"the Alpha and the Omega." In 1:17, the risen
Christ is "the first and the last." It probably is in this
vein that the whiteness of head and hair, which one
might expect of "the Ancient of Days," is ascribed
to "One like a Son of Man," that is Christ.

The point in Revelation probably is not to stress
age, but it is significant that in this awesome picture
of the risen Christ, a physical mark normally implying age is a positive ascription to the Savior and Lord
of the Church. This is in striking contrast to television ads which see grey hair as bad, calling for some

subtle dye which will remove this "give away" of
the unpardonable sin of getting old! If Revelation
does not eulogize age, neither does it apologize for it.
Revelation finds no problem in portraying the Savior and Lord of the Church with white hair.

Another affirmation of age in Revelation may be
found in the prominence of "the twenty-four
elders," featured a dozen times in chapters 4—5; 7;
11; 14; 19. Already we have observed that the term
"elder" represented an office in Jewish life, prominent in the affairs of synagogues and Sanhedrin, and
in the early churches. As observed, "elder" came
gradually to designate the office more than actual
age. However, seniority was requisite when the office arose, and it never lost completely this reference. Although there is no direct reference to age in
the prominence of "the elders" in Revelation, the
very term and its original force are on the side of
esteem for age, with no necessary denigration of
youth.

In summary, the minimum implication from Revelation is that there is no rightful place for denigrating age in the church. A strong case can be made for
the rightful esteem of age and its right to prominence, even at levels of authority. The Lord of Church
and world is one whose head and hair are "white as
wool, white as snow." The "twenty-four elders" are
never identified in Revelation, but throughout they
occupy positions of prominence. They may typify the
twelve patriarchs of Israel and the twelve apostles of
the church, thus symbolizing the reconstituted Israel
of God. This is a likelihood, not a certainty. In any
event, they represent something positive and
esteemed in the church.

7

Age in the Writings of Paul

Paul was a crusader from first to last. Before his conversion to Christ he lashed out against Stephen and other Christians, trying to wipe out the movement (Acts 8:1-3; 9:1-2; Gal. 1:13; Phil. 3:6; 1 Tim. 1:13). After his conversion to Jesus as the Christ, he crusaded for human freedom, rights, and responsibilities. His vision of a new humanity "in Christ" ruled out any discrimination or favoritism such as may be based upon ethnic, legal, or sexual difference: "There is not any Jew or Greek, not any slave or free person, not any male and female, for all of you are one in Christ Jesus" (Gal. 3:28). This stance was based upon Paul's understanding of the grace of God. Paul saw life itself as the gift of God's grace (Rom. 6:23), and salvation is God's free gift, not a human achievement or reward for merit (Eph. 2:8-10). To Paul, any dependence upon human work or merit is a repudiation of grace. To set one person above another on the basis of such human works as circumcision was to Paul nothing less than to be "fallen away from grace" (Gal. 5:4). To Paul it was "either-or." Salvation was either the free gift of God's grace or a deserved reward for human merit or achievement. This is what Paul meant by "falling from grace," to turn from dependence upon God's goodness to one's own goodness.

This is the key to Paul's "egalitarian" principle. All are sinners and have earned "death" as "the wages of sin" (Rom. 6:23). Before God there is no really significant distinction between Jew and Gentile, slave or free, male or female. Paul was not denying the reality of ethnic, legal, and sexual differences. They obviously are realities. His point was that the very idea of grace excludes any proper practice of favoritism or discrimination. Each person has worth, freedom, rights, and responsibilities as the gift of God's free grace.

Paul fought openly and throughout his Christian life against the legalism which would give advantage to Jew over Gentile, to circumcision over uncircumcision (see Rom. 2:25-29; Eph. 2:11; Col. 2:11). He openly resisted any disposition to discriminate against Gentiles or uncircumcised persons, as to both salvation and such privileges as table fellowship (Gal. 2:11-14). He not only called for humanizing principles in master/slave relationship (Eph. 6:5-9; Col. 3:22 to 4:1); but in Philemon he called for something more radical, that a master receive back his runaway slave Onesimus not as a slave but as a brother! Paul made great strides in implementing his new vision as to women, although his practice was somewhere between the ideal of Galatians 3:28 and the customs of the culture and piety of his times.[1] Paul's principle would call for the rejection of discrimination against any person based upon stereotype or the distinctions of race, nationality, sex, or legal status. What about age?

It may come as a surprise and a puzzle that Paul seems to have said little directly on the subject of age. We have seen this already with respect to Jesus. No one has done so much for human dignity

and freedom as Jesus, and Paul was a faithful fol-
lower of Jesus in human liberation. One answer may
be in the fact that in Judaism age was honored, and
it was not there that Jesus and Paul found it necessary to fight for human rights. Of course, we have
no complete record of what either said on any subject. In what we do have, there is nothing negative
toward age; and there is much that is positive toward
age. Probably the chief answer is in the fact that
both Jesus and Paul recognized human rights and
responsibilities to be universally the gifts of God's
love, and both saw good and evil in terms of inner
qualities, not in terms of outward distinctions of
family lineage, cultic rites, or anything arbitrary or
superficial. They gave themselves in sacrificial service for all humanity. Had "agism" been a problem
comparable to "racism" or "sexism," they probably
would have addressed this problem more directly
and more emphatically.

Respect. Paul did have a good bit to say on the
subject of age. He called for respect for age, but
he also called for respect of youth. In the Pastoral
Epistles especially (1 and 2 Tim.; Titus),[2] considerable attention is given to age groups. An "older
man" is not to be rebuked, rather he is to be ex-
horted *(parakalei)* as one would exhort a father (1
Tim. 5:1). The same Greek word served for "elder"
and "older man," but the context here favors age as
such and not office. There is a clear recognition here
that age does not insure against fault, and an older
person may need to be admonished. The point is that
it is to be done with due respect for age. Although
age is often abused by the aged, it is seen as something which in its own right calls for respect. "Older
women" (in Greek the feminine form for "elder")

likewise are both to be respected and to be admonished as occasion requires. "Older women" are to be admonished as one would admonish a mother. The egalitarian principle holds in this context, with old and young to be treated as family: treated like a father, a mother, a brother, a sister. Love, respect, and responsible care are assumed.

In 1 Timothy 5:17 "elders" who "preside well" are to be judged worthy of "double honor." These are older men who have some "ruling" authority in the church. What is meant by "double honor" is not specified, but the context implies material support: "The worker is worthy of his wage" (v. 18). By this time the churches were developing more structures, and "elders" were paid, especially for "laboring in the word (preaching) and in teaching" (v. 17). The context allows the "double honor," presumably material support, on the basis of age or competence, but the latter seems to be stressed. On the negative side, "elders" may be found at fault; but care should be taken that they not be accused lightly: "Do not accept a charge against an elder except upon the basis of two or three witnesses" (v. 19). This is not to imply that unfounded charges should be heard against anyone, old or young; but special care should be exercised where already one's character has been established. This should not say anything negative against youth, but it should be a reminder that one should not forever have to be answerable to rumors or idle tongues. If there is evidence supported by two or more witnesses, older people are as responsible as any to meet the charges. Of course, if an older person has a record of wrong doing, that record itself is a factor in matters of judgment and discipline. Where there is no negative record, age has the right to freedom from the harassment of idle tongues. Again, this is not to overlook the rights of any age to fairness and the assumption of innocence until the evidence to the contrary are substantive.

That older men and older women are vulnerable is clearly assumed in Titus 2:2f., where both are called to responsible and mature deportment: "But as for you, speak what things are fitting to sound teaching; older men to be temperate, serious, sensible, sound in faith, in love, in steadfastness. Older women likewise in reverent behavior, not slanderers nor enslaved to much wine, teachers of what is good. . . ." The very call to positive qualities implies that older men and older women are vulnerable to negative qualities, some of which are specified. Pressed strictly as a code, these admonitions could be problematic for just about anyone. It is not apparent that older women are more susceptible to gossip or heavy drinking than older men; and older women as well as older men need to be sound in faith, love, and steadfastness. The passage is best taken in terms of its mood or spirit, not as a rule book. As such, it openly recognizes both the vulnerability of older men and women to fault and failure; and it clearly recognizes that positive compliance with good is proper and possible to older men and women. To call older people to responsible living is not to imply that younger people are not likewise called to such quality of life. This passage addresses the special responsibilities which come with age.

If age is to be respected, so also is youth. Twice in Paul's letters is youth singled out for respect, in both cases relating to Timothy. Timothy's age is not known to us, but he seems to have been a young man. Age is relative, and to Paul, Timothy was a

young man (1 Cor. 4:14-17; 2 Tim. 2:2). Writing the
Corinthians, Paul said, "If Timothy should come, see
to it that he comes to you without fear, for he does
the work of the Lord as I; do not let anyone despise
him (count him as nothing or belittle him). Send him
forth in peace, in order that he may come to me, for
I await him with the brothers" (1 Cor. 16:10f.).
Timothy's age is not mentioned here, but it is explicit in another reference: "Let no one look down on
your youth, but be an example for believers in word,
in manner of life, in love, in faith, in purity" (1 Tim.
4:12). At Corinth, the problem may have been in the
character of the Corinthians, unrelated to age. In the
latter passage, the clear implication is that a young
minister could be given less than due respect simply
because he was young. Paul rejects this "agism"
both by condemning the prejudice against youth
and by calling young Timothy to the highest quality
of responsible and mature life and ministry.

That some temptations are especially perilous to
youth is implied in 2 Timothy 2:22, "Flee youthful
desires; pursue righteousness, faith, love, and peace,
along with those calling upon the Lord out of a pure
heart." Presumably, implied are temptations to sen-
suality. That such are not exclusive to youth is well
known, for old people are vulnerable, too. It probably follows that the pressures upon young people
are normally greater than upon older people in this
regard. It is not "agism" to recognize successive
stages in life; it is agism and stereotype to absolutize,
for example dividing sins up into two separate
classes: sins of youth and sins of age. The text before
us simply in a practical way cautions youth against
what age should know about already.

Maturity: Paul made much of maturity, as in his

appeal to the Corinthians: "We speak wisdom among
those who are mature, not the wisdom of this age nor
of the rulers of this age who are doomed to pass
away. But we speak God's wisdom" (1 Cor. 2:6-7).
Paul found true wisdom not in the self-seeking or
self-serving dispositions of the world but in the love
which came to its greatest expression in Christ,
"God's power and God's wisdom" (1:24). The cross,
with its self-giving love is seen as the focal point in
history for such wisdom and power. Whatever else
may have belonged to "maturity" for Paul, it would
be shaped by God's wisdom.

Paul did not limit maturity to the aged, but he saw
age as properly on the side of maturity. Christians
should not remain babies, fed milk instead of solid
food (1 Cor. 3:1f.). He clearly thinks of immaturity in
terms of infancy or childhood and of maturity in
terms of adulthood. However, Paul wrote 1 Corinthians to adults, not to children. Maturity to him is
not simply a matter of age, even though he can use
chronological ages as models. To Paul, maturity is a
matter of quality of existence, not calendar years. To
be mature is to be "spiritual" (living under the
claims of God) and not "carnal" (living apart from
God). Jealousy and strife, such as plagued the Corin-
thian church, are "flesh" and not "spirit" (3:3). Spiritual maturity is a matter of condition, not age as
such. Even so, it is an adult quality to be mature and
infantile to be immature. This is not agism; it is the
recognition that maturity is something to be attained and that it does not come automatically with
age. It comes in response to the calling of Christ
Jesus as Savior and Lord. It comes as a growth experience in Christ.

This same maturity is seen in Ephesians as the

goal of Christ's continuing ministry in and through the church. The living Christ gives various "equipping ministries" to the church so that these ministers may equip all the saints for the work of ministry (4:11-12). The goal is that the whole church become a "perfect man" or "mature man" (v. 13). The Greek word *(teleios)* is the same as that in 1 Corinthians 2:6. The "mature" are contrasted here as in Corinthians with "babies": "That we no longer be babies" (Eph. 4:14). Again, it is not chronological age but condition which is intended. The mature are not vulnerable to "every wind of doctrine" that blows, but they are grounded in truth (reality) and love in Christ (vv. 14-16). Again, maturity is not automatic with age. Old people may be immature and young people may be mature, but age should be on the side of maturity.

Death. The proverb has it, "As sure as death and taxes." Physically we are all dying. Death comes eventually to all, and death is just a heartbeat away for anyone at any age. Insurance companies fix premiums on established life expectancies for different age groups. These actuaries are reliable for insurance purposes, but they tell nothing about the individual. They represent life expectancy for the "average" at a certain age, but not even the physician knows an individual's life expectancy. Physical death is a reality, and it is one with which any meaningful life must cope. Paul knew how to cope with death. Paul has much to say to all of us about death, whatever our age.

Paul did not fear death, nor did he grow weary of life. He attained a wholesome stance in which he was prepared to accept death and also to accept life with its opportunities. His most beautiful expression of his own ability to affirm life or death is in Philippians: "To me to live is Christ and to die is gain" (1:21). Paul was under arrest and awaiting trial for his life when he thus wrote. He was awaiting a trial in which he could be freed or executed. If released, he would return to the very work out of which his arrest arose (v. 22). Death would mean being with his Lord, and for him that could only be gain. His response was significant: "What I shall choose, I do not make known" (v. 22). Translations which have Paul say "I know not" go against all evidence. Paul had a word for "know" and used it often. The word he employs should be rendered, "I do not make known" (see 4:6; 1 Cor. 12:3; 15:1; Gal. 1:11). Paul was attracted to both life and death, for each held the promise of meaning for him, whether continuing ministry in life or being with Christ in death. It was his responsibility and privilege to make the most of whichever came, not to carry the burden of which it should be. In Shakespeare's play, Hamlet loathed life as empty and feared death as an unknown. He did not want "to be or not to be." Paul found both options attractive and was willing to accept each in its proper time.

Death may be a frightening threat to young or old. It is normal for the young to want to live, and many old people see life as completed and want death to come. Impairments and pain can make this acute. But there also are young people who find life empty and want no more of it, and there are old people who try desperately to hang on, no matter what their physical condition. If anything is clear it is that attitudes toward life and death are not something to be put off as long as possible. It is never too soon to prepare oneself for either eventuality, life or death.

In earlier years as a Christian, Paul may have expected to live until Christ's return. He writes as though he would be among the living at the return of Christ: "For the Lord himself with a shout, at the voice of an archangel and at the trumpet of God, will come down from heaven, and the dead in Christ will arise first; afterwards, we the living, those remaining, shall be caught up together with them in the clouds unto a meeting with the Lord in the air, and thus we shall be with the Lord always" (1 Thess. 4:16-18). However Paul is to be understood here, at least later he saw clearly that he might die at any time before the return of Christ. He was able fully to cope with the prospect of death, something which he faced many times (see 2 Cor. 4:7-12; 11:21-33). He learned to live daily with the dangers of imprisonment, shipwreck, robbery, persecution, hunger, sickness, etc.

How did Paul do it? How did he attain such poise in the face of the demands of both life and death? He would say, "Christ!" For him Christ had become all. Yielding all he gained all. Claiming nothing, he had everything (Phil. 4:10-13). In one sense, the resources were within himself. In another sense, they were in Christ. Paul knew an inner sufficiency only because Christ within was his sufficiency. He had found life by losing it. He had found meaning in servanthood. No doubt Paul yet knew the impulse to rule (see 1 Cor. 16:1-4, where if Paul decides to go to Jerusalem, the committee will go with him; he did not go with anyone!). Paul continued to have to do battle with himself, as he made plain (see Rom. 7; 1 Cor. 9:24-27; Phil. 3:12-16). Paul thus knew life as a continuing struggle even with himself, but he also knew in Christ the resources for coping both with life and the prospect of death.

Aging should be on the side of coping with death, but Paul's kind of maturity and poise does not come automatically. Primarily, it is as one finds meaning in life that one finds preparation for death. In part this comes with such assurance as Paul had that there is a fuller life awaiting one beyond death, including a redeemed body through the resurrection (cf. 1 Cor. 15:3-58). In fact, Paul expected the creation itself to be redeemed and renewed in a way paralleling the redemption of the resurrected body (Rom. 8:18-25). However, it was not just this hope for the future which sustained Paul. Life here and now must have meaning, else life beyond death holds no real promise. Paul was not just marking time until death. Life already was fulfilling for him (Phil. 4:18). In the later years of old age, such a view of life and death is to be desired. To have it then makes it urgent that in the earliest years one be open to the values, principles, and commitments which give life its meaning, now and beyond death.

Paul, an old man. Philemon is an amazing letter. Striving desperately to free both a slave and a master, Paul bared his heart in many ways in this little letter. He sought to free Onesimus from the dehumanizing status of a slave. He sought to free the slave's master from the dehumanizing status of a slave-owner. He sought to liberate both slave and master into the dignity and freedom of Christian brothers. Paul so identified with the slave that he made the owner's acceptance or rejection of Onesimus the acceptance or rejection of himself (v. 17). At one point, Paul made his appeal on a personal basis, with probably a special reference to his own advanced age: "Wherefore, having much boldness in

Christ to command you to do what is required, because of love I beg you instead, being such a one as Paul an old man *(presbytēs),* now also a prisoner of Christ Jesus—I beg you for my child, whom I begat in my bonds, Onesimus" (vv. 8-10).

Paul's word here is not the familiar *presbyteros,* "elder." It is a kindred word *presbytēs,* which normally referred to an old man, an aged man. Some scholars have speculated that Paul used the word here for "ambassador," but its normal usage fits well. The context strengthens the case for normal usage, for Paul has just said that he will not command but appeal. He is not commanding in the role of "ambassador" but appealing as "Paul, an old man," in jail and begging for the liberation of his "child." There are rightful claims which age may have, and Paul had earned the right to press the claims of "an old man" upon a slave's master. If Paul does here use his age to bring pressure to bear upon the slave owner, it was not in a self-serving way. Paul was asking for something for himself, but chiefly he was pleading for the humanity of a slave and his master. Paul is not presuming in any selfish way upon the privileges of age; he is bringing the power of his years to bear upon a situation in a redemptive way.

That Paul was at least somewhat advanced in age is not dependent simply upon Philemon 9. He probably was in his fifties and sixties when he wrote the letters remaining to us. His actual age cannot be established, but he already was a young man when Stephen was stoned to death (Acts 7:58), probably not long after the death of Jesus. What is more important than the actual age of Paul is the direction of the life. Paul appears at his worst in his youth, both by the witness of Acts and Paul's own confessions (Acts 8:1-3; 9:1-2; Gal. 1:13; Phil. 3:6; 1 Tim. 1:13). As a youth he was proud of his superiority, number one in his class (Gal. 1:14). His zeal was so misinformed and misguided and his mind so closed that he was coercive and intolerant of any disagreeing with his inherited faith. He actually dragged men and women out of their homes to publically punish them (Acts 8:3). In one of his earliest letters, he confessed with anguish, "I persecuted God's church violently and tried to destroy it" (Gal. 1:13). Although even his Christian life continued to be a struggle by his own admission (Rom. 7; 1 Cor. 9:24-27; Phil. 3:12-16), he did mature. He grew in his understanding of the Christian calling, and he grew as a person. He must have been around sixty years of age when he wrote Philippians from jail, and there is not a whimper in the letter. There is joy, gratitude, faith, and hope; but there is no trace of self-pity, fear, bitterness, or complaint. With his chain, he has everything (4:18)!

The letter of 2 Timothy is a beautiful reflection of what old age can be. This letter is a deeply moving one. What does he have to say from jail? There is gratitude for others. There is prayer for others. There is encouragement for others, including this: "Suffer hardship with me as a good soldier of Christ Jesus" (2:3). In the face of likely imminent death, his courage is firm: "Faithful is the word, if we suffer together, we also shall live together, if we endure, we also shall reign together; if we deny, that one also will deny us; if we prove unfaithful, that one will remain faithful, for he is not able to deny himself" (2:11-13). He warns against betrayal of the faith, and he encourages the ongoing of faithful work.

Sensing that his time is short, he is prepared for his departure (4:6-8). He does want the company of his friends: "Do your best to come to me soon" (4:9). He wants his cloak and his books, especially the parchments, presumably Scriptures (4:13). Again, he pled, "Do your best to come before winter" (v. 21). In earlier life, friends meant much to Paul. Now Paul, an old man, repeats the plea, "Do your best to come." If we could hear them, many are making the same plea, not necessarily from jail but from the loneliness of wherever they are, the old home, nursing home, or wherever: "Do your best to come!"

8

Age in the General Epistles

Grouping Hebrews, James, 1 and 2 Peter, and Jude admittedly is a convenience. The practice is common and is followed here. These writings have no common authorship, nor do they come from one school. They are varied in content, in perspective, and otherwise. The twenty-five verses of Jude in their brevity do not address the subject of age. The other four writings will be treated separately.

Hebrews

The major concern of this writing is to encourage the readers to press on into the fuller freedom and meaning of the Christian faith. The temptation or tendency to linger too much in aspects of their Jewish background is faced as a major threat to their fulfillment. The past is affirmed for its proper meaning and role, but the readers are challenged to move on in their ongoing pilgrimage in Christ. Much use is made of the model of shadow and reality, ancient rites having foreshadowed the realities now experienced in Christ.

A focal word (and its cognates) in Hebrews is "maturity," sometimes rendered "perfection." The word group is built upon the Greek *telos*, most simply rendered "end." Usually the term is used for "end" in the sense of goal. "Maturity" comes nearest in English to capturing the idea. Christ himself is "perfected" or brought to his completion through suffering service (see Heb. 2:10; 5:9; 7:28; 12:2). What the Mosaic law or temple rituals could not do, Christ does in "completing," "perfecting," or bringing those who trust him to their "goal," "maturity," or "perfection" (see 5:14; 6:1; 9:9; 10:1,14; 11:40; 12:23). Significant for our study is what has been seen in earlier writings, that maturity has no necessary correlation with age, but age should be on the side of maturity. In Hebrews, as elsewhere in Scripture, immaturity is thought of under the model of "baby," whereas maturity is thought of under the model of a growing or grown person. The very fact that in Hebrews, as elsewhere, the readers are warned against immaturity and called to maturity implies that calendar age does not of itself determine the matter. The readers are assumed to be adults in calendar age, not necessarily grown or mature as persons.

Agism may appear to be present in passages like Hebrews 5:11-14, where the immature person is censured as remaining "a child" (v. 13); but this does not stand up under careful reading. The writer does not fall into the stereotype which finds young people immature and old people mature. To the writer, maturity is a condition, not an extension of years. These scolded are told that "because of the time" (v. 12), that is, length of time since their conversion, they should now be teachers. Instead, they yet need to be taught the ABC's of God's word, yet requiring milk instead of solid food. Enough time has transpired that they should be mature enough to teach, but in fact they are so immature that they must be fed like little children. Clearly, then maturation is not simply a matter of aging; it is personal growth bound up with such personal factors as faith, openness, commitment, and effort.

Old people can be "babies" through their own default in the face of opportunity. The writer is not considering involuntary cases, as where genetic factors or accident may render one retarded or incapable of maturation. The letter is addressed to people who can read or understand the letter as written, not to those involuntarily incapacitated. These are the people who can be aging chronologically but not maturing as persons.

There is no implication that little children are to be faulted for being little children. It is normal and proper that an infant be given "milk" and not "solid food." Immaturity is normal and proper to a little child. What is not proper is for immaturity to continue in a person capable of maturation. Thus, there is no "agism" or stereotype here. With aging we may not necessarily mature, but we should mature. Where we have options, as with the readers of Hebrews, to linger in immaturity is inexcusable.

A further lesson from the great concern in Hebrews for Christian maturity is that maturity cannot be imposed. The writer could only warn and plead; he could not command maturity. Even Christ, "the pioneer and perfector of our faith" (12:2) can only lead and call; he cannot coerce maturity. The proverb has it, "You can lead a horse to water, but you cannot make him drink." The writer of Hebrews recognizes that you can offer a person the word of God, but you cannot make him think. Even the land upon

which the rains fall may bear either useful "vegeta-
tion" or only "thorns and thistles" (6:7f.).

James

James scorned religion which made creed a substitute for deed. To those proud of their orthodoxy, he
gave the reminder that even the demons are mono-
theists, believing that "God is one"; but they only
shudder at the thought (2:19). James did not teach
human works as a substitute for faith; he called for
the kind of faith which validates itself in what it pro-
duces. He did not falter in his insistence upon saving
faith, but he distinguished it from mere creedal be-
lief. He did not offer works as an option to faith; he
insisted that the genuineness of faith could be observed only in the works which followed from it. By
works he meant such as care for the widow and
orphan along with personal purity (1:27) and minis-
tering to human need wherever it is encountered
(see 2:14-17; 5:1-6).

Paul and James were not in conflict; they dealt
with different situations. They meant the same
thing by "faith," openness to God as we meet him in
Jesus Christ. To them faith is trust. They meant different things by "works." By "works" Paul meant
such ritual acts as circumcision, in no way saving.
By "works" James meant what Jesus and Paul
meant by "fruit" (see Gal. 5:22). Both James and
Paul followed Jesus in the teaching that what one is
comes to expression in the outward patterns of life.

James not only called for the faith which pro-
duces; he called for maturity. He went directly to
this concern early in the letter: "Let steadfastness
have its work perfected, in order that ye may be per-

fect, whole in every way, lacking nothing" (1:4).
James did not expect "perfection" in the popular
understanding of that term. He called for maturity,
that one reach one's potential. Nowhere does James
link maturation directly to age. As is the pattern in
the Bible, maturity is bound up with personal attitudes and commitments which are independent of
age, appearing in some persons but not in others,
whatever the age. Faith bearing the fruit of good
works; grateful recognition that we live out of the
goodness of God; sensitivity to the needs of other
people and active response to those needs; self discipline, especially of the tongue; freedom from the
tyranny of desire; realistic acceptance of human
limitations; steadfastness and hope; these and other
such qualities are ingredients to James for fulfillment. Age should favor such but does not guarantee
such. Whether young or old, these are the qualities
to cultivate for meaningful life.

James finds human failure, at whatever age, in
several directions; but one passage in which he
sharply etches the features between life fulfilled and
life unfilled reads thus: "Who is wise and understanding among you? Let him show out of the good
manner of his life his works in the gentleness of wisdom. If ye have bitter jealousy and selfish ambition
in your hearts, do not boast and do not be false over
against the truth. This is not the wisdom which
comes down from above, but it is earthly, secular
(unspiritual), demonic. For where jealousy and strife
are, there are instability and every vile practice. The
wisdom which is from above is first of all holy, then
given to peace, gentle, open to persuasion, full of
mercy and good fruits, impartial, unhypocritical; for

the fruit of righteousness is sown in peace by those making peace" (3:13-18).

There is much more in James, but this captures much of what to him is the maturity of authentic faith and fulfilled personhood. He does not prescribe it for the aged in particular; and if such is to be known in the senior years, it should be giving shape to life already in the early years.

At one point James makes explicit reference to age, in pointing to one role of "the elders of the church" (5:14). In this passage, the elders are to be called upon when there is sickness and where "the prayer of faith" (v. 15) or "the prayer of a righteous man" (v. 16) avails much in its power. It does not necessarily follow that this to James is the sole role of "the elders" or that only "the elders" are effectual in prayer for the sick. The passage does assume some major role for "the elders of the church," including such crisis experiences as illness.

James makes much of the transitory nature of human life, it being like a mist which appears and then quickly disappears (4:14). James is not cynical about life. He is not afraid of its brevity or its being subject to a quick ending. He points to the transitoriness of life to warn against the presumption of being able to control the future, as though one can really anticipate what he/she will do today or tomorrow (4:13). To James it is an evil and arrogant boast to presume to control the future (v. 16). Instead, James would have us live daily in the realistic recognition of our frailty and our dependence upon God, whom already he has shown to be the source of every good and perfect gift (1:17). James is especially harsh with the presumption of the rich that by their riches they can control their destiny, reminding the rich man that he can fade away as quickly as the scorching of grass or flower under a burning sun (1:9-11). James' point is not to empty life of hope or to fill it with despair. His concern is to free us from false hope, empty faith, and meaningless life. Even the transitoriness of life and the frail grip which we have upon physical life need not rob life of its meaning or victory.

Significantly, James does not relate the contrasting lives and destinies to age. Wealth is a peril to the one who puts his/her trust in it, whatever the age. Disappointment and defeat await any who think that apart from God they can control the future, whether one is young or old. James does not write in order to instruct in aging or for age, but his letter gives the basic values, principles, and conditions for meaningful life, be the years few or many.

First Peter

This letter clears at least one point for us: "the elders" are older people and not just people of any age with an office so designated (1 Pet. 5:1-5). The elders are contrasted with those who are "younger" (v. 5). Precise ages distinguishing "the elders" and those who are "younger" are not given, but at least chronological age is implied. The elders also have some recognized responsibility and corresponding authority. They are told, "Shepherd the flock of God among you" (v. 2); and "the younger" are told to "be subject to the elders" (v. 5). Although roles are thus recognized, care is taken to safeguard against abuse. Elders are to look after (episkopountes) the flock not by necessity but with a voluntariness which they have in their relationship with God (v. 2). They are to assume such a pastoral role not for shameful gain but with commitment to the task, not in a domineering way but as examples for the flock and with the recognition that elders and all alike are under the ultimate care of the chief Shepherd. Elders and the younger alike are to be clothed with humility, characterized by the grace which belongs to the humble. The roles, then, are functional, not designed to elevate one person as such above another person. Authority is not vested in elders or others as such; authority is matched to responsibility. The only authority which one may have over another is that authority without which responsibility cannot be discharged. No person is to be above another person, but some roles are to be subordinated to other roles. This is in all structures of life: ball teams, businesses, churches, or whatever.

The writer identifies himself as a "fellow elder" (5:1). The only credentials he singles out are those bound up with age as well as experience: "a witness of the sufferings of Christ and a partner in the glory about to be revealed." In the letter, the writer does draw upon a past not directly accessible to the readers. His readers had not seen Jesus (1:8). The writer does not live in the past, but he has lived long enough to inform the present by drawing from the past. Writing to Christians under the threat of severe persecution, his own past has prepared him for guiding them through this crisis, he having been "a witness to the sufferings of Christ." The "elder" does have unique credentials for ministry. He is especially qualified to admonish those tasting persecution for the first time: "Beloved ones, do not think

it a strange thing that these fiery trials have come
among you, as though a strange thing were happen-
ing to you" (4:12). Many have been through such
fiery trials before and have survived, and this
"elder" is one such.

If the past can inform the present, there is a special place in ongoing life for those old enough to have
experienced something of the past. In Galatians,
where the conflicts were chiefly within the church
itself, Paul was blunter than the "elder." Paul closed
that letter with a curt warning to anyone concerned:
"Henceforth let no man trouble me; for I bear on my
body the marks of Jesus" (Gal. 6:17). In effect, Paul
said, "Get off my back!" He had earned the right to
be spared being hounded by people who could not
match him in his years of suffering for Christ, including the bearing of literal scars from many beat-
ings. In 1 Peter, the "elder" writes with more re-
serve, but the same authority of personal experience
through the years equips him uniquely for helping a
persecuted church through a new crisis of persecution.

In 1 Peter as in James, the transitoriness of
human life is recognized; and as in James, life in the
flesh is seen as vulnerable to death as are grass and
flower (1:24). This recognition that all physical life
moves toward death is not in a defeatist mood;
rather it is the foil against which the Christian's new
birth is seen as not of "perishable seed but of imperishable, through the living and abiding word of God"
(v. 23). This is the "good news" which is preached.
The writer styles himself an "elder," but he is not
intimidated by the brevity of life nor by its inevitable movement toward physical death. This should

be the confidence of older people to whom death is near. It should be the confidence of young people, for death to them, too, is always a near neighbor.

Just having acknowledged the fragile nature of physical life and having affirmed faith in the good news of being "born anew" from "imperishable seed," the writer immediately issues a challenge to maturation (2:1-3). He recognizes that the "new born" Christians must begin with "spiritual milk," but they are expected as nourished to "grow up into salvation" (2:2), that is, into the fuller dimensions of salvation. Again, there is no agism or stereotype in which one age group is as such proper or improper, positive or negative. Maturation is a normal process and should begin at birth and continue throughout life. It is proper for a baby to be a baby, but it is when older people remain babies that life has failed.

Second Peter

Although disputed by much scholarship, this letter identifies itself as from "Simon Peter, slave and apostle of Jesus Christ" (1:1). What is significant for our purpose is that the writer further identifies himself as one who knows that the putting off of his body will be soon (1:14), presumably in view of old age. It is the writing of a man of some age. The letter is a positive witness to age as experienced or as perceived.

Ascribed to a man expecting to be not long "in this body," the letter reflects none of the stereotype commonly associated with old age. The writer knows the past and can draw upon it, but he is not living in the past. He can reminisce, but he does so only to reinforce the present or point to the future. He has not terminated his pilgrimage nor muted his call to maturation. Trusting in the "precious and great promises" of God and knowing the threat of the "corrupt desires in the world" (1:4), he issues the call to march ahead: "And for this very reason, bringing to bear all diligence, provide in your faith virtue, in your virtue knowledge, in your knowledge self-control, in your self-control steadfastness, in your steadfastness godliness, in your godliness brotherly love, in your brotherly love love" (1:5-7). Without a trace of "dotage," this writer scorns such arrested growth as renders one "ineffective or unfruitful" or "blind and shortsighted" (vv. 8-9), calling upon his readers to validate their "call and election" (v. 10). Salvation to this writer, apparently advanced in years, is not static but dynamic. His pilgrimage in faith continues and he calls others to the march.

These are qualities which stereotype customarily attributes to youth. They in fact belong to individual disposition, transcending age. Young or old can march under the sign of "Exodus," moving ever from bondage to the promised land. Young or old can remain bogged down in Egypt, unequal to the Exodus. It is agism and stereotype to see it otherwise. Young or old can respond to or be deaf to the call: "Let us therefore go outside the camp to Him, bearing his reproach, for we do not have here an abiding city, but we seek a city which is to come" (Heb. 13:13-14). Churches today which deny voice to youth in its assemblies or trusted leadership to the young because they are young do disservice to all. By the same token, churches afraid or unwilling to call to highest levels of leadership ministers who are beyond fifty are uninformed by history and blinded by the stereotypes of agism. Writings like 2 Peter did not come from a children's day camp. The right to be heard belongs to those having something to say, not those in a certain age bracket, young or old. The right to positions of leadership belongs to those able to lead, not a restriction dictated by the date on a birth certificate. Many young people suffer because they are not trusted until proven, and they cannot prove themselves until trusted. Many older people are laid on the shelf because someone looked at the birth certificate but failed to look at the person. Agism hurts everyone, young and old, those who practice it and those against whom it is practiced. Unless we are prepared to cut out of our biblical canon books written by persons over thirty, or forty, or fifty, or sixty, or whatever age, we ought to cut out agism. It could well be that letters like 2 Timothy and 2 Peter were written by persons past "retirement age"! Who knows?

9
Summary and Conclusions

Age. Chronological age, aging, and agism are related but not identical. Calendar age may be computed from a birth certificate. "Young" and "old" are relative, depending upon "compared to what." Calendar age is no certain clue to physical, mental, emotional, or moral condition. Quantity and quality of life do not always go hand in hand.

Aging. Growing older? Guess who? That's you. That's me. That's us. The grammar here is not the best, but the fact is incontestable. All of us are growing older—from birth to physical death. Not even medical science really understands why bodies age, but they do. Ponce de Leon's search for the Fountain of Youth remains unsuccessful, but science has not given up and yet seeks to discover the cause and cure to aging.

Aging does not just become a problem in old age; for some there is more trauma in turning 30 or 40 than in turning 60 or 70. Many children want to be older than they are, and many adults want to be younger than they are. Some people go through life wanting to be older until they switch to wanting to be younger, never knowing the joy of being what they are. This identity crisis is a proper concern for young and old, not just for the elderly. A daily column poses the question, Why grow old? The obvious answer is that the alternative is to die young. The question implies that "old" is bad, a dogma which needs to be examined. Aging should be on the side of maturity, wisdom, goodness, and fulfillment. Sometimes it is and sometimes not. The kings Saul and Solomon got worse with age: Jacob and Paul got better.

Agism. Like racism and sexism, this is a major problem. It is the practice of stereotype, assuming that all people of a given age are alike. This is a one-factor analysis, where one looks at a person's birth certificate but not at the person. Agism lets calendar age override all other factors, even though it may be minor in comparison.

Anyone of us may be guilty of practicing agism. Some agism is open and vicious, some subtle or unintentional. Even the sophisticated can be guilty. An example appears in *Time* (23 June 1980), where "gerontocracy" is found to be a major problem in the Soviet Union's failure to change for the better: "So each board member hangs on and on, becoming increasingly shortsighted as he becomes increasingly sclerotic" (p. 29). It would be more cogent to observe that these mean old men were like that when they were young. It is simplistic agism to reduce the evils of any system to the issue of age. Old people can be crabby, incompetent, and mean. They can be the opposite. David Ben-Gurion and Golda Meir were advanced in years when they gave Israel some of the nation's best leadership. Moses at 80, Aaron at 83, Caleb at 85, and Joshua about the same comprised a "gerontocracy" in Israel's early history, and they were not "shortsighted" or "sclerotic." Winston Churchill was in his older years when he lifted Britain out of what seemed to be her doom

during World War II. Young and old may be "sclerotic" or not. Saul of Tarsus was at his worst as a
young man: proud, bigoted, coercive, intolerant,
with a closed mind. Only a traumatic conversion
turned him in a new direction. If Paul was ever
"sclerotic" it was in youth and not in his senior
years. Both physical and mental sclerosis can come
early or late. Jack Ossofsky put it well: "It is not so
important to know how old you are as it is to know
how you are old."[1]

The older generation. There is a growing awareness of the particular problems of becoming older.
Churches and communities need to be sensitized, informed, and enlisted in positive concerns for older
people and for conditions favorable to growing older
gracefully. Informed concern should include problems of loneliness, sense of meaning, retirement, role
exit, material needs, psychological needs, social
needs, legal needs, and spiritual needs. Such specif-
ics as daily phone contact with home bound persons,
transportation (church, shopping, pleasure), legal
assistance (tax forms, wills, etc.), handyman helps
around the house, information service as to agencies
designed to serve the elderly—these and countless
other matters belong to responsible relationship
with older people, seen not as problems but as persons.

Senior adults already constitute a major segment
of society, and their numbers doubtless will increase.
According to *Life* (December 1978), there were
5,000 centenarians on Social Security in 1971. There
were 4,842,000 octogenarians in the U.S.A. in 1978.
From Harvard's 1919 class of 683 graduates, 208
octogenarians survived as late as 1978. Charlie
Smith, born in 1842 and sold as a slave in New Or-

leans in 1854 as a 12-year-old boy, was alive and well at age 136 as this book was in preparation. There is no known reason why the human life span should be limited to 70, 80, 120, or whatever.

Biblical perspectives. In the span of many centuries covered by the Bible, it is not surprising that different perspectives appear on age and aging. Prevailingly, old age is esteemed. Age is not often a deliberate subject, but there are some direct and significant treatments of the subject. That age received less attention than many other subjects probably implies that discrimination against older people was not a major problem in Judaism and early Christianity. If either, age was more favored than youth, although generalization here is extremely precarious. At least, there was no "cult of youth" as in much modern society.

As stereotype and one-factor analysis, agism denies a human being his/her basic and God-given right to be oneself, the right to one's own individual identity. Agism is the injustice of viewing all children, all teen-agers, all young people, all middle-aged people, or all senior persons as alike.

Stereotype. Our language abounds with prejudicial expressions: "senile," "an old fogey," "a dirty old man," "kid stuff," etc. We hear it said, "You can't trust a person over 30." Others say, "You can't trust a person under 30." One is said to be "set in his ways," usually implying an oldster. To others, "Life begins at 40." All of this is agism and simplistic stereotype. Indeed, you can't trust some people after 30, and probably they could not be trusted before 30. You can't trust some people before 30, not because they are under 30 but because of their individual qualities. Competence is found in some young people and in some old people. Incompetence is all around us, found among all ages. Life begins for some at 40, for some earlier, for some later, for some never.

In biblical perspective and in observable evidence, there is no necessary correlation between quality of life and length of life. The direction of a life and not its duration is decisive for its quality. It is not how long but how one lives that matters most. If the direction of a life is wrong, it does not help to speed up or just keep going. The quality of life improves with aging or deteriorates with aging, depending upon what qualities are built into it: attitudes, disposition, values, principles, goals, purpose, etc.

In biblical perspective and incontestably, the best time to get ready to be old is as soon as possible. Most people, and certainly anyone able to discuss the subject, can have much to do with choosing what kind of persons they will be in the older years. Beauty and power in the senior years do not just happen. They are not accidents. One in the early years largely determines what the later years are like. In his old age King Saul was filled with bitterness and fear, but these negative qualities were predictable. Despite positive factors in his youth favorable to a meaningful life, Saul over a period of years chose what led inevitably to the emptiness of his old age and his eventual suicide. On the other hand, Jacob is an example of one who became a much finer person in his older years. This did not just happen. For all his early trickery and self-serving ways, he did look to God and finally through great trauma was brought to a change so great that Jacob the supplanter became Israel, Prince of God.

Change for the better can come late in life, as in

the case of Jacob. In biblical teaching it is clear that the longer one follows the wrong way the harder and less likely it is that he/she will turn to a better way. One can reject the light so long that eventually one destroys the power to see (John 9:39). On the other hand, there is no determinism or fate to which one must submit. Nicodemus can be born again, even when old (John 3:4). Probably no lesson from our studies is more urgent than this one: change for the better may come at any stage in life, but the best time to get ready to be old is when one is yet young.

There are voluntary and involuntary factors in human existence. Some things are beyond our control. Time itself is not subject to our wills. Time moves on, eventually taking each one to physical death. Time through wear and tear can diminish one's powers or finally destroy them. Genetic factors can cause impairment of body or mind, striking at any time from birth to death. Accidents and disease can close in upon a life, imposing conditions beyond our control. These are among the involuntary factors which may shape a life, in youth or age. There also are voluntary factors, and these are the ones with which we are properly concerned. If we can read these lines or talk about this subject, we can do something about the quality of our existence. We can do something to determine what kind of person we shall be in the older years. We can begin by rejecting the stereotypes of agism which write one off simply on the basis of a birth certificate.

The generation gap.   By biblical evidence, the generation gap is not new. That young and old are different is normal and right within proper limits. That they sometimes are more divided by a gap than bound together for mutual advantage is neither necessary nor good. In some hospitals today the parents and newborn baby are given a room to themselves for the first hour following the baby's birth, this for "the bonding" of the family. This is good! Beyond this, the generations should be "bonded," not victimized by a "generation gap." Unfortunately, there are neglect, discrimination, and abuse practiced between youth and age.

The generation gap may be vicious or innocent. The story of Elisha and the 42 boys mangled by two bears illustrates the generation gap with a vengeance (2 Kings 2:22 f.). The boys reduced the old prophet to a bald head, and he was so insecure and threatened that he sought to destroy them. David and Solomon illustrate the generation gap without malice, yet the gap was painfully there. David found it hard to pass on the torch to his son Solomon, especially in the building of the Temple (1 Chron. 22-29). There was affection between the two, yet the relationship was made difficult for both as David continued to treat Solomon as a boy long after Solomon had become a man. The gap is not one-sided.

In biblical perspective, the generations can be bonded rather than divided. Such was true of Naomi and her daughters-in-law Orpah and Ruth. Naomi gave them full freedom and encouragement to rebuild their lives following the deaths of their husbands. Orpah and Ruth found different courses, but both related positively and supportively to Naomi. Where there could have been a growing gap, they built bridges and strengthened bonds.

In biblical perspective, older persons should be neither neglected nor abused. Today they are both neglected and abused in many cases. In one survey, of those over 60 and not in institutions, 27% were

found to be *enjoyers* of their senior years, 53%
were found to be only *survivors*, and 20% were
found to be *casualties*, unable to cope with life.[2]
Behind this situation are some involuntary factors
beyond control. Importantly, there are voluntary
factors which could increase the number of *enjoyers* and move at least some of the *survivors* and
casualties up to a higher level of meaning and fulfillment.

Unfortunately, there is not only neglect of older
people but actual abuse. Much of this comes from
the older children and other relatives of the elderly.
To many, the older person is seen more as a problem
than a person. It is not uncommon for older people to
be insulted, berated, hated, and physically abused.
Ironically, two major problems today are child abuse
and the abuse of the elderly. Child abuse is such that
currently the federal government has budgeted
sixty million dollars to combat it. It may be that the
problem of the abuse of the elderly is equal to that of
child abuse. The Bible has no kind word for people
unkind to children or the elderly.

Retirement. Trauma or joyful harvest? For some,
retirement is a multifaceted problem; for others it is
a joyous blessing. For the taxpayer it is an increasing burden. For retirees it may be a blessing or a
trauma. Some older people are in position to retire
and can do so without inconvenience, without a
sense of guilt (as though one must continue to "produce" or forfeit the right to be), and without a sense
of emptiness (as though life has no meaning apart
from work). For them retirement is not the end of
life but the beginning of a new chapter in life with
new options. For others retirement is traumatic.
Some find themselves locked into a fixed income out-

run by inflation. Some find nothing to replace work, giving them a sense of having no worth.

One answer to retirement is found in a biblical pattern allowing for flexibility (Num. 8:23-26). The Levites had a modified retirement, with reduction of work load but not total withdrawal from active service. No plan is fail-safe, but there is here a principle for implementation. Retirement need not be a "Babylonian Exile." There could be flexibility both as to calendar age and degree of involvement. "All or nothing" is not an unbreakable law.

Retirement is most problematic for older people when arbitrary, forced, and total. The community could be served by the gifts of older people, and older people could be given happier options. Moses, Aaron, Joshua, and Caleb—all above 80—were not retirees; and they served their nation well. Zechariah, Simeon, and Anna were old, but they served the Christian movement at its rise. Older people should not hold on in such a way as to deny due opportunity to younger people, but neither should they be shunted off by nothing else than a birth certificate. Probably no retirement plan can be devised once-for-all, but there can be openness to the matter and constant review.

Growing older gracefully. Much can be done in preparation for more meaningful older age. One thing is to be realistic and positive about the limits of physical life. Physical death is universal and but a heartbeat away from any one of us from infancy to actual death. It is a positive thing to take our mortality into our self-affirmation. To be physically mortal is a part of who we are. This need not be a "morbid" attitude taken with defeatist resignation. It can be salutary to see that as to physical life, all any of us has right now is now. Past and future have their proper places and importance, but in youth and older age we can try to make *now* count.

We may have the assurance of life beyond physical death, a basic Christian assurance, and that in itself should be a sustaining factor; but life should have meaning here and now. Fullness of life is possible now, transcending the fluctuations of physical factors. The fruit of the Spirit is love, joy, peace, patience, kindness, goodness, faith, gentleness, and self-control (Gal. 5:22). These are the qualities which can enter into a life and give it direction and meaning. These qualities cannot be imposed upon us, but they are there for us if we are open to God and these qualities. Such qualities can make the difference between being *enjoyers* or just *survivors* or *casualties* in the later years.

The Beatitudes in the Sermon on the Mount are highly instructive as to factors which largely determine the quality of life, in youth or old age. Jesus declared "blessed" or "happy" persons characterized by such qualities as meekness, hunger and thirst for righteousness, mercifulness, purity of heart, peacemaking, and the willingness to suffer for the sake of Christ and of what is right. The list is not exhaustive, but it points out the direction of meaningful life. If one wants to grow old gracefully, with beauty and power, these are among the qualities which must be built into life, and the earlier the better.

Nothing has so much to do with the quality of life and its fulfillment, whether young or old, as the principle which Jesus made primary. If we try to save ourselves, we self-destruct; if we are willing to lose ourselves to God and other people, we find life (John 12:25). Like a grain of wheat, one must "die" to "live" (v. 24). To be selfish, turned in upon oneself, guarantees failure. Nothing so damages human existence and makes the later years emptier or more miserable than garden-variety selfishness. On the other hand, just look around at the older people whose lives are radiant in power and beauty. They are not selfish people. They are people who have found life by giving it to God and to the service of other people.

Dr. T. B. Maston, the writer of the Foreword of this book, is such a person. This is why we "drafted" him to write the Foreword. At 83 years he is not as strong physically as in earlier years, but in his great personal qualities he is a joy to know. Dr. Maston did not just happen to grow older gracefully. He and Mrs. Maston, and others like them, have beauty and power in their older years because early in life they gave themselves to the values, principles, goals, and relationships which yield such quality of life. They cultivated the attitudes and disposition which produce such quality of life. They gave themselves to the Christ who can give life and give it abundantly. People like these have found life by giving it to others. That is much of the "secret" of how to grow older gracefully and meaningfully.

Another factor in growing older meaningfully is the willingness to accept the God-given right to be oneself. Life is gift, and the right to be oneself is gift. We do not have to earn the right to be. We had nothing to do with being born into the world. We are not responsible for being here, but in being here we are responsible. One of our responsibilities is to accept ourselves and our right to be. Have you ever heard an adult say to a child, "If you are ever going to amount to anything!" This implies that the child does not amount to anything now. It implies that one does not have worth until earned. This goes against the biblical doctrine of creation and the biblical doctrine of grace.

Added to this is that dogma in our tradition which insists that each day we must do something to prove again that we have the right to be here. This is disastrous for many older people, for whom forced retirement or impairment means that they are no longer able to "produce." Many thus feel worthless. Work should be a joyous privilege, an open opportunity to anyone able to work. Older people should have the right not to work when work is no longer a positive factor for them. Older persons need to be assured of and to accept the right to be — to be themselves with security, dignity, and meaning.

Work is not to be an end in itself, else one becomes a "workaholic."[1] Work is proper as a means to serving other people and/or as personal fulfillment. Older people who can work and want to work should have the opportunity to work. Older people who want to rest from work should be privileged to do so with dignity and security. Persons were not made for work, but work has meaning as it contributes to human fulfillment.

Peace with oneself is essential to any age. This means self-acceptance and self-affirmation. At any age, one should be open to growth and betterment, but there is a wholesome acceptance of oneself, "warts and all." This includes acceptance of one's age, whatever it is. There is good news for us all. It is all right to be young, and it is all right to be old! Just as it was a victory for black people when they and others came to recognize that "black is beautiful," so it is right for us to recognize that "old, too, can be beautiful!"

Notes

CHAPTER 1

1. See also George E. Burch, cardiologist, Tulane Medical School, quoted by Elsie Martinez, "Do You Have to Grow Old?" in "Dixie," *The Times-Picayune* (18 May 1980), pp. 32-35.

2. See also Gerhard von Rad, "Deuteronomy," *Interpreter's Dictionary of the Bible* (Nashville: Abingdon Press, 1962), A-D, p. 834, who observes that the Passover traditionally was "celebrated as a feast by local family units" but was transformed by Deuteronomy into a "pilgrimage feast" celebrated at one common place.

3. G. Vermes, *The Dead Sea Scrolls in English* (New York: Penguin Books, 1977—2nd. ed.), p. 111.

4. See also R. H. Charles, *The Apocrypha and Pseudepigrapha of the Old Testament* (Oxford: Clarendon Press, 1913), vol. 2, p. 48.

5. N. H. Snaith, "Numbers," *Peake's Commentary on the Bible* (New York: Thomas Nelson and Sons, 1962—rev.), p. 257.

6. Ibid.

7. See G. Henton Davies, "Elders in the Old Testament," *The Interpreter's Dictionary of the Bible* (Nashville: Abingdon Press, 1962), E-J, p. 72ff. for possible solution.

8. See also von Rad, p. 834.

9. Ibid., p. 837.

10. See John D. W. Watts, "Deuteronomy," *Broadman Bible Commentary* (Nashville: Broadman Press, 1970), p. 260, for helpful insights on this difficult passage.

CHAPTER 2

1. I owe attention to this passage to J. Robert Nelson in remarks made in a conference concerned with a different issue.

CHAPTER 3

1. See also Evelyn and Frank Stagg, *Woman in the World of Jesus* (Philadelphia: Westminster Press, 1978), pp. 79-84.

CHAPTER 4

1. See Page H. Kelley, "Isaiah," *Broadman Bible Commentary* (Nashville: Broadman Press, 1971), vol. 5, pp. 149-374 for a careful review and assessment of options as to the origin, structure, background, and interpretation of the book.

2. Robert B. Laurin, "Lamentations," *Broadman Bible Commentary* (Nashville: Broadman Press, 1971), vol. 6, p. 205.

3. See A. S. Kapelrud, "Gebal," *The Interpreter's Dictionary of the Bible* (Nashville: Abingdon Press, 1962), E-J, p. 359f.

4. John Joseph Owens, "Daniel," *Broadman Bible Commentary* (Nashville: Broadman Press, 1971), vol. 6, p. 386. See this commentary for excellent survey of options and interpretations.

5. Ibid., p. 374f.

6. L. H. Brockington, "Jonah," *Peake's Commentary on the Bible* (Nashville: Abingdon Press, 1962), p. 627.

7. A. J. Glaze, Jr., "Jonah," *Broadman Bible Commentary* (Nashville: Broadman Press, 1972), vol. 7, p. 181.

8. John Patterson, *The Goodly Fellowship of the Prophets* (New York: Charles Scribner's Sons, 1948), p. 117f.

9. Ibid., p. 116f.

10. Raymond Calkins, *The Modern Message of the Minor Prophets* (New York: Harper & Brothers, 1947), p. 91.

11. Gordon Pratt Baker, *The Witness of the Prophets* (New York: Abingdon-Cokesbury Press, 1948), p. 63.

12. Patterson, p. 220.

13. See also G. Vermes, *The Dead Sea Scrolls in English* (New York: Penguin Books, 1975—2nd ed.), p. 132f.

14. Jacob Milgrom, "Studies in the Temple Scroll," *Journal of Biblical Literature*, vol. 97, no. 4 (December 1978), p. 514.

15. John D. W. Watts, "Zechariah," *Broadman Bible Commentary* (Nashville: Broadman Press, 1972), vol. 7, p. 317.

16. Calkins, p. 112.

CHAPTER 6

1. See R. Alan Culpepper, *The Johannine School*, SBL Dissertation Series 26 (Missoula, Montana: Scholars Press, 1975).

2. See Frank Stagg, "The Abused Aorist," *Journal of Biblical Literature*, vol. 91, no. 2 (1972), pp. 222-231.

ING

CHAPTER

1. See E ... *l of Jesus* (Phila...

2. These ... con- tests and d ... let- ters as bein...

CHAPTER

1. Jack ... New York (Cleve...

2. Resea ... icana Healthcare ... AP New York (...

3. See V ... *The Facts Abou...*